안녕

HELLO from KOREA

안녕!

HELLO from KOREA

1994, 1997, 1998, 1999 Fourth Edition

Copyright l999
Written by Jeannie J. Park, Edward J. Park,
Sylvia R. Chwe, Beckhee Cho, and others
Design and Photo Selection by Shin S.Sam
Illustrations by Kim Jae-Sung Studio

Published by
Korean Overseas Culture and Information Service
Seoul, Republic of Korea (ROK)

Printed by
Jungmoonsamoonhwa Printing Company, Ltd.
208 -10 Songsan-dong, Map'o-gu, Seoul, Korea

This book was published to promote international
understanding and knowledge of the Republic of Korea.
The authors alone are responsible for
the opinions expressed in this book.

ISBN 89-7375-359-2 43910

Dear Readers:

As friends would say to each other in greeting, 안녕 (*an-nyŏng*) or hello! Depending on the formality of a situation and the respective ages of the friends, 안녕 can take several forms and encompass several meanings, but in this book, take it in the way we mean: a heartfelt welcome to Korea.

A nation is only as strong, rich and vibrant as its people. Too often, however, slogans and statistics are all we know about other countries, with little impetus to find out more.

Test yourself. What comes to mind when you think of Korea? You might visualize the 1988 Olympics, through which many foreigners got their first exposure to this country. How about a dish of spicy kimchi? A shiny white Hyundai car? Or simply a tragic map of a peninsula, divided in two.

As stereotypes the images have served Korea fairly well, but flush with newfound prosperity and confidence the nation seeks to tell its story on its own terms. And what a long, rich, tragic, even comic, story it is.

Although this book does not purport to be the most comprehensive volume, we do hope that you will find it a good companion, a source that may answer questions you'd ask of a Korean person if you could.

Sincerely,

The Authors

Contents

●The Tan-gun Myth

Once there was a divine prince named Hwanung, who was the son of Hwanin, the God of the Heavens, Hwanung wanted to help mankind, and asked his father to grant him the Korean Peninsula to govern. Hwanin granted his wish, and Hwanung was sent to Earth with three thousand followers.

Hwanung appeared near a divine sandalwood tree on the slopes of T'aebaeksan Mountain. He took the title of Ch'ŏnwang or "Heavenly King" and established Shinsi, the City of God. He appointed three ministers to be in charge of wind, rain and the clouds, and taught the people 360 useful arts including agriculture, medicine, carpentry, weaving and fishing. He also taught them what was good and evil, and set up a code of law.

In those days, there were a bear and a tiger who were living in a big cave near the sandalwood tree where Hwanung had become human, and so every day they went to the sacred sandalwood tree and prayed to Hwanung. Eventually, the Heavenly King was moved by their prayers.

He called them to him and gave them twenty bulbs of garlic and a divine spray of mugwort, and said, "Eat these, and do not seek the light of day for one hundred days. If you do this, you will become human."

The bear and the tiger ate the garlic and mugwort and went back to their cave. The tiger was too impatient to survive this ordeal and left after a short while. Meanwhile, the bear patiently waited and after only twenty-one days, she became a beautiful woman. She became known as Ungnyŏ.

The woman was overjoyed, but she could find no one to marry her, and so she visited the sandalwood tree again and prayed that she might be blessed with child. Hwanung again took pity on her, and temporarily transformed himself into a human. She conceived, and later gave birth to a son, who was called Tan-gun.

The people of the country rejoiced at his birth, and later he became the first human king of the peninsula. He established his capital at Pyongyang and he gave his kingdom the name Chosŏn. Later, he moved his capital to Asadal on T'aebaeksan Mountain and ruled for 1,500 years. After that, he abdicated and became a mountain god.

Korea in Brief

Land and Climate

The Korean Peninsula extends southward from the northeast part of the Asian continent. The Peninsula is currently divided into the Democratic People's Republic of Korea (DPRK) in the north, and the Republic of Korea (ROK) in the south. To the west of the Peninsula lies the Yellow Sea, with China on the other side. Japan lies across the East Sea, and the Pacific Ocean lies to the south. The country has a varied terrain, with about 70 percent being mountainous, particularly on the east coast. The western and southern coasts are deeply indented, and there are more than 3,000 islands and harbors. The major rivers on the peninsula include the Amnokkang River (Yalu, 790km) and Tuman-gang River (Tumen, 521km) in the north and the Naktonggang River (525km) and the Han-gang River (514km) in the south. The highest mountain on the Peninsula is Mt. Paektusan (2744m); Mt. Hallasan (1950m) on Chejudo Island and Mt. Sŏraksan (1708m) are two of the more well-known mountains in the south.

Korea enjoys four seasons and a variety of different weather types. Spring and autumn are rather short, but very pleasant with crisp weather and many days of sunshine. Located in the East Asian monsoon belt, the peninsula has hot, humid summers, with the main rainfall occurring during the monsoon season which usually begins at the end of June. Winter is cold and dry, with occasional snow, although spells of cold weather normally alternate with days of warmer weather.

Official Name : Republic of Korea (ROK).
Area : of total peninsula: 222,154 Km^2; of ROK: 99,392 Km^2
Location : between latitudes 33^0 and 43^0 North and longitudes 124^0 and 131^0 East.
Population : 45,991,000
Facts **Capital :** Seoul
Other Major Cites : Pusan, Taegu, Taejŏn, Kwangju, Inch'ŏn and Ulsan
Monetary Unit : Won.

People

The Koreans are one ethnic family speaking one language. They share certain distinct physical characteristics which differentiate them from other Asian peoples including the Chinese and the Japanese, and they have a strong cultural identity as one ethnic family. The modern Korean people are believed to be the descendants of several Mongol tribes which migrated onto the Korean Peninsula from Central Asia particularly during the Neolithic Age (c. 5000-1000 B. C.) and the Bronze Age (c. 1000-300 B. C.). By the beginning of the Christian era, the Koreans were a homogeneous people, although the country was not politically unified until the seventh century A.D.

The population of the Republic of Korea topped 45.9 million in 1997. Its population density is among the world's highest, and Seoul, the capital city, has more than 11 million inhabitants. Other major cities include Pusan,Taegu, Inch'ŏn, Kwangju, Taejŏn and Ulsan. In recent years,

Korean Language

The Korean language is spoken by more than 65 million people living on the peninsula and its outlying islands as well as 5.5 million Koreans living in other parts of the world. The fact that Koreans all speak and write the same language has been a crucial factor in their strong national identity. Modern Korean has several different dialects including the standard one used in Seoul and central areas, but they are similar enough that speakers do not have trouble understanding each other.

Linguistic and ethnological studies have established that the Korean language belongs to the Ural-Altaic group of Central Asia, which also includes Turkish, Hungarian, Finnish, Mongolian, Tibetan and Japanese. Korean, like Japanese, also includes a rich vocabulary borrowed from Chinese in the same way that many European languages include a large number of words of Latin and Greek derivation. *Han-gŭl*, the Korean alphabet (originally called *Hunmin-chŏngŭm*) was invented in 1446 by King Sejong and his court, and consists of 10 vowels and 14 consonants which are used to form numerous syllabic groupings. *Han-gŭl* is easy to learn and write, which has greatly contributed to the high literacy rate of Koreans.

Consonants: ㄱ ㄴ ㄷ ㄹ ㅁ ㅂ ㅅ
k/g n t/d r/l m p/b s/sh

ㅇ ㅈ ㅊ ㅋ ㅌ ㅍ ㅎ
ng ch/j chʹ kʹ tʹ pʹ h

Vowels: ㅏ ㅑ ㅓ ㅕ ㅗ ㅛ ㅜ ㅠ ㅡ ㅣ
a ya ŏ yŏ o yo u yu ŭ i

How do you do?

안 녕 하 세 요

ㅇㅏㄴ ㄴㅕㅇ ㅎㅏ ㅅㅔ ㅇㅛ
an nyŏng ha se yo

Celebrating Buddha's birthday

A ritual celebrating Confucius's birthday

urbanization has been increasing, although the government is taking steps to minimize this trend. The traditional extended family stystem is giving way to the nuclear family.

Religious freedom is provided for in the Korean Constitution, and Koreans have taken to religion with a fervor. Some 51 percent of the public holds religious beliefs, and that figure continues to grow. The major religions include Buddhism, Protestantism and Catholicism.

Constitution & Government

The Republic of Korea was officially established on August 15, 1948. The Republic has a democratic form of government based on the separation of powers and a system of checks and balances as prescribed in the Constitution, which was promulgated on July 17, 1948. There are three branches of the government: the executive, the legislative and the judiciary.

At the head of the executive branch is the President, who is elected by direct popular vote to a single five-year term.

The President performs his executive functions through the State

Mass being read in a Korean Catholic church (left). Youngnak Presbyterian Church (right).

Council, which consists of himself as chairman, the prime minister as vice-chairman, and the heads of 17 executive ministries. The prime minister is appointed by the President with the approval of the National Assembly.

There are several organizations to aid the President and the State Council. They are the National Security Council which is chaired by the President and whose regular members include the Prime Minister and concerned executive ministers, the Advisory Council on Democratic and Peaceful Unification and the Presidential Council on Science and Technology, the Planning and Budget Commission, the Presidential Commission on Women's Affairs and the Presidential Commission on Small amd Medium Business. The Board of Audit and Inspection, under the direct jurisdiction of the President, is responsible for auditing the accounts of central and local government agencies, state-run corporations and related organizations.

Legislative power is vested in the National Assembly, a unicameral body. Currently, the National Assembly consists of 253 members who are elected by popular vote to a four-year term, and 46 members selected in a proportional representation system among political parties winning five or more seats in the direct election.

The judiciary system is three-tiered, with the Supreme Court at the top, three appellate courts, and district courts in the major cities. The Supreme Court examines and passes final decisions on appeals of the decisions of appellate courts in civil and criminal cases. Its decisions are final and indisputable, forming judicial precedents.

Economy

Over the last three decades, especially since Korea launched its First Five-Year Economic Development Plan in 1962, its economic growth has been among the fastest in the world. In 1996, Korea joined the OECD and took a step closer to becoming an advanced nation. Korea's per capita GNP stood at over US$10,000 at the end of 1996. Some factors generally cited to explain the "Miracle on the Han-gang River" include strong government support, the export-oriented economic strategy, the emphasis on high-technology in industrial policy and the abundance of highly skilled and educated labor.

These impressive accomplishments have been overshadowed recently by the difficulties facing some of Korea's large business groups and financial institutions. Business failures, coupled with the financial crisis sweeping through Asia since July 1997, raised doubts among foreign investors and led to a serious liquidity crisis in December 1997.

To help solve the crisis, Korea and the International Monetary Fund reached an agreement on a bail-out program in December 1997. Since then, then there have been dramatic reforms which have effected banks--some of which were closed down--big corporation, and government agencies. Now the Korean economy is back on the right track and international rating agencies are restoring Korea's good credit rating.

The major industries of the Korean economy include electronics, textiles, petrochemicals, steel, automobiles and shipbuilding. The chief agricultural products are rice, barley, wheat, potatoes, and vegetables with 21 percent of the land being arable. Mineral products include tungsten, coal and graphite. The major exports are electric and electronic goods, textiles, steel, petrochemicals and automobiles; the major imports include petroleum products, iron and steel, electrical machinery, textiles, machinery, chemical products and grains. The Republic's biggest trading partner is the United States, followed by Japan and then China.

Education

The Korean education system basically consists of elementary schools (six years), middle schools (three years), high schools (three years), and colleges and universities (two to four years) with graduate courses leading to Ph.D. degrees. Elementary education is compulsory for children aged six to 11. The basic elementary school curriculum is generally divided into eight subjects: Korean language, mathematics, social studies, science, ethics, physical education, music and fine arts. Students in middle school are required to take a number of additional subjects, such as English, and can take electives, such as technical or vocational courses. Afterwards, students can choose between general education and vocational high schools. In general, high school tends to be rigorous, as the competition for college admission is notoriously stiff.

A Typical Middle School Student's Schedule

Name: Huh Jung-won   Class: 3-17

	Monday	Tuesday	Wednesday	Thursday	Firday	Saturday
8:20-9:15	Individual Study					
Period 1 9:15-10:00	Homeroom	Korean	Industrial Arts/ Home Econ.	Korean	Physical Education	English
Period 2 10:10-10:55	Mathematics	Ethics	Mathematics	Industrial Arts/ Home Econ.	Music	Natural Science
Period 3 11:05-11:50	Korean	Natural Science	Korean	History	Sociology	Korean
Period 4 12:00-12:45	Physical Education	English	Physical Education	Natural Science	Biology	
12:45-1:30	Lunch					
Period 5 1:30-2:15	English	Industrial Arts/ Home Econ.	Fine Arts	English	Chinese Characters	
Period 6 2:25-3:10	Ethics	Sociology	Elective	Mathematics	Mathematics	
Period 7 3:20-4:05	History			Homeroom	Industrial Arts/ Home Econ.	

History

Legend has it that in 2333 B. C., a semi-divine being named Tan-gun founded a kingdom called Chosŏn on the Korean Peninsula (see p. 5). Koreans regard that year as the founding of the Korean nation. In the more than 4,000 years since then, the Korean people have been a model of consistency in preserving traditional concepts and values and yet quickly and skillfully adapting to changing circumstances. While this brief chapter cannot hope to do justice to the richness of Korean history, we hope that the reader will be able to learn about some of the events which helped formed this nation.

The Beginning

Scholars generally believe that the earliest kingdoms or states on the Korean Peninsula first began to form during the Bronze Age (1000 B.C.-300 B.C.). Of these, the kingdom supposedly founded by Tan-gun, generally known as Ko-Chosŏn or Old Chosŏn, soon emerged as the strongest, becoming consolidated by the beginning of the fourth century B.C.

As Old Chosŏn's strength grew, China became more and more concerned. The Chinese Emperor Han Wuti launched an invasion in 109 B.C. and destroyed the kingdom the following year. Four commanderies were established to administer the northern half of the Peninsula.

Within a century, though, a new kingdom called Koguryŏ (37B.C.-A.D. 668) emerged in the northern half of the Peninsula. Koguryŏ was a nation of warriors, and led by aggressive and valiant kings such as King Kwang-gaet'o (r. 391-410). It conquered neighboring tribes one after another, expanding in virtually every direction. It was Koguryŏ which finally drove the Chinese out of their last commandery, Nangnang (Lo-lang in Chinese), in A.D. 313. At its height, its territory thrust deep into Manchuria and stretched well into the southern half of the Korean Peninsula.

A new kingdom named Paekche (18 B.C.-A.D. 660) developed south of the Han-gang River in the vicinity of present-day Seoul. The people of Paekche were more peaceful than the ferocious warriors of Koguryŏ, and they moved south to avoid the threat of their northern rival. By the fourth century, Paekche was firmly established as a prosperous and civilized state, trading extensively with its overseas neighbors. In fact, Paekche served as an important

The tombstone for Koguryŏ King Kwanggaet'o (r. 391-413), built in 414 in Tong-gou, Jian city, Jilin province in China, proves that the territories of the Koguryŏ Kingdom (37 B.C.-A.D. 668) extended well into what is now northeastern China. (above)
A hunting scene drawn on a sixth-century mural painting from a Koguryŏ tomb. (left)

bridge for the transmission of mainland culture to Japan, passing on Buddhism, Chinese characters, and political and social institutions. A Paekche scholar named Wang In even served as teacher to the Japanese Crown Prince.

Shilla (57 B.C.-A.D. 668), farthest from China, was at first the weakest and most underdeveloped of the three kingdoms. The last to adopt foreign creeds and ideas, its society was markedly class-oriented. It later developed remarkable power, drawing resources from its unique *Hwarang* (Flower of Youth) corps and Buddhist teachings.

By the mid-sixth century, Shilla had consolidated its power and territory and entered into a military alliance with T'ang China to subjugate both Koguryŏ and Paekche. The Shilla-T'ang forces were successful, and the Peninsula was unified for the first time in A.D. 668. Following this, the survivors of the Koguryŏ Kingdom repulsed T'ang forces

Royal tombs in Kyŏngju, the capital of the Shilla Kingdom (57 B.C.-A.D. 935) (above)
Bronze incense burner (Paekche) (left)

in Manchuria and the northern part of the peninsula and established the Kingdom of Parhae in 698.

Although politically separate, the three kingdoms of Koguryŏ, Paekche and Shilla were related ethnically and linguistically. Each of them developed a sophisticated political structure and legal system and adopted Confucian ethics and Buddhist faith.

Kim Yu-shin
(595 - 673)

In the Shilla kingdom, talented young men were chosen to be members of the *Hwarang* or "flower of youth" corps. They trained together in academics (philosophy, classics, morals), the military arts (horseback riding, swordsmanship, archery and strategy) and the cultural arts (poetry, painting, music and dancing). They followed five rules set by the famous Buddhist monk Wŏn-gwang: 1) to be loyal to the king; 2) to obey one's parents; 3) to be faithful to one's friends; 4) to never retreat in battle and 5) not to kill unless necessary. It was through the efforts of the *Hwarang* that the peninsula was unified, and among them, Kim Yu-shin was the best.

Considered to be the greatest Shilla general, Kim Yu-shin won some spectacular victories which allowed Shilla to unify the country. Born an aristocrat, Kim Yu-shin dreamed of becoming a great warrior and began military training from a young age. He joined the *Hwarang* at the age of 15, and by 18, was considered a master swordsman. He fell in love with a kisaeng (a female entertainer similar to the Japanese geisha), which turned out to have a tragic ending. Unable to concentrate on his studies he went over to visit her every night. His mother found out about this and reprimanded him severely, so he decided to abandon his lover to continue his studies. One day, however, after returning from a training session he fell asleep on his horse. The horse, accustomed to stopping by the kisaeng's house every day, took Kim there. Upon waking up, Kim was outraged and in front of his lover, killed his horse to make sure he would never return again to her. His lover killed herself, and Kim went off to train by himself in the mountains for seven years.

When he emerged, he quickly demonstrated his skills, and was soon made a commander in the Shilla army. By the time Shilla had become allied with the T'ang China forces in 655, Kim was in command of the Shilla forces. They captured the capital of Paekche in 660, and in 668, they were finally able to defeat Koguryŏ.

Kim Yu-shin was well rewarded for his efforts by the king and lived comfortably until the ripe old age of 78.

Unified Shilla and Parhae

For two and a half centuries, Shilla enjoyed peace and prosperity. Freed from the worries of domestic conflicts and external invasions, it achieved rapid development in the arts, religion, commerce, education and all other fields. The Shilla capital, present-day Kyŏngju, had a population of over one million and boasted magnificent royal palaces and Buddhist temples.

Buddhism flourished under the patronage of the nobility and court, exerting tremendous influence upon state affairs, artistic creation and ethics. Some of Korea's outstanding historical monuments are attributed to the creative genius and religious fervor of the artisans of this time. Among them are Pulguksa Temple and Sŏkkuram Grotto Shrine, both located in the vicinity of Kyŏngju.

Tabot'ap Pagoda in Pulguksa temple (Shilla)

Shilla reached the peak of its prosperity and power in the mid-eighth century, but gradually declined thereafter. Conflicts among the nobility intensified, while rebel leaders claimed succession to the demolished dynasties of Koguryŏ and Paekche. In 935 the king of Shilla yielded power over to Wang Kŏn(posthumous name, King T'aejo), founder of the Koryŏ Dynasty.

Parhae's political system resembled that of T'ang, and its capital Sanggyŏng was modelled on the T'ang capital Chang-an. Its distinctive culture drew from both T'ang and Koguryŏ. When Parhae was overrun by the Khitan in the beginning of the 10th century, its ruling class took refuge in the newly established state of Koryŏ.

Koryŏ

The founding monarch of Koryŏ (918-1392), Wang Kŏn, was a general who had served under a rebel prince of Shilla. Choosing his native town Songdo, the present-day Kaesŏng (located about 60km north of Seoul), as the seat of his kingdom, he proclaimed a policy to recover the lost territory of Koguryŏ in Manchuria. Therefore he named his kingdom Koryŏ, from

23

Kŭnjŏngjŏn, the throne hall in Kyŏngbokkung Palace.

which the modern name Korea is derived.

From the outset, the royal court of Koryŏ adopted Buddhism as the state religion. It flourished greatly, stimulating temple construction and the carving of Buddhist images as well as icon paintings. But temples and monks came to wield excessive power, and during the kingdom's later years, conflicts between scholar officials and warriors and between Confucianists and Buddhists weakened the kingdom. The Mongol incursions which began in 1231 resulted in its occupation of Koryŏ for nearly a century.

Chosŏn

Confucianism was introduced in Korea around the beginning of the Christian era, almost at the same time as the earliest written Chinese material entered the peninsula. However, it was not until the Chosŏn Dynasty (1392-1910) that Confucianism began to dominate Korean society.

The founder of the Chosŏn Dynasty, Yi Sŏng-gye (posthumous name, King T'aejo), used the influence of Confucian intellectuals to help him overthrow the Koryŏ Dynasty. He relocated the capital from Kaesŏng,

King Sejong the Great
(1397 - 1450)

Only one king in Korean history has ever been deemed worthy enough to have been accorded the title "the Great." That king was the fourth king of the Chosŏn Dynasty, King Sejong, who is universally regarded as the wisest and most gifted ruler in Korean history. The long list of accomplishments during his reign is astonishing, to say the least, and probably no other time in Korean history was quite so creative and productive.

As a child, Sejong was a quiet, studious boy who showed an avid love of learning. He was enthroned when he was 21. During his reign, a renaissance in art, literature and science began.

A patron of the arts and sciences, he attracted around him the very best minds of his day. He established the Chiphyŏnjŏn or a Hall of Worthies early in his reign. The best scholars in the land gathered here to pursue research and study, and many of the notable achievements during Sejong's reign can be attributed to the close cooperation between Sejong and them.

Sejong was a practical person, who took a keen interest in the day-to-day affairs of government, tenaciously seeking ways to improve the lives of his citizens. He reformed the tax system and constantly tried to refine the government. During his reign, major progress was made in virtually every field: agriculture, astronomy, defense, diplomacy, geography, literature, medicine, printing,

science—you name it.

King Sejong's greatest accomplishment however, is the creation of *Han-gŭl*, the Korean alphabet. Aware that the general public needed a writing system besides the complicated system of writing in Chinese characters, the king and his Hall of Worthies devised a simple alphabet that could be easily learned.

Originally called *hunmin-chŏngŭm* or "correct sounds for the instruction of the people," *Han-gŭl* consisted of 28 letters (now there are only 24—see p.11) which were modeled after the shape of the vocal organs. It has been widely praised as one of the most scientific alphabets in the world by many and still remains a source of great pride for most Koreans.

This was not the only important invention of his reign. A new calendar, a pluviometer (an instrument to measure rainfall), an anemoscope (an instrument to measure wind speed and direction), sun dials, water clocks, models and instruments to study heavenly bodies, astronomy charts, atlases, new printing types—the list goes on and on.

In these ways and many others, King Sejong strengthened the nation and brought peace and cultural vitality, which is more than anyone could ask of even a king. He helped shape Korean society and culture into what they are today, and his influence on politics, ethics, history, music, literature, and the sciences, and especially the language, is still felt today. He died on the 17th day of the Second Moon of 1450, having ruled the nation for 32 of its most glorious years.

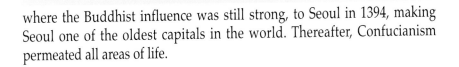

where the Buddhist influence was still strong, to Seoul in 1394, making Seoul one of the oldest capitals in the world. Thereafter, Confucianism permeated all areas of life.

The Choson rulers governed with a well-balanced, sophisticated political system, based on Confucian principles of ruling and administration. To become a government official, one needed to take the *kwago* civil service examination, which tested people on the Chinese classics.

Confucianism also determined the rigid social structure. The society in general valued academic learning highly while disdaining commerce and manufacturing. At the top was the *yangban* or scholar-aristocrat class which dominated government, the military, and society. Next was the *chungin* or "middle people" consisting of professionals such as government functionaries, doctors, lawyers, and artists. Below them were the *sangin* or commoners, which formed most of the population. They were mainly peasants who were given land to farm. Merchants and artisans were also in this class. At the bottom were the *ch'onin*, the serfs, servants or slaves who were considered low-born or outcasts.

The high point of the Choson Dynasty is generally considered to be the reign of King Sejong (r. 1418-50), Choson's fourth monarch. During his reign (see p. 25) Korea enjoyed an unprecedented flowering of culture and the arts including the invention of *Han-gul* the Korean alphabet, as well as numerous inventions and progressive ideas in the areas of government administration, economy, the natural sciences, the humanities, music and medicine.

In the late 16th century, however, a horde of Japanese invaders led by the warlord Toyotomi Hideyoshi overran most of Choson, on its way to invading China. Most of the peninsula was devastated, and numerous cultural treasures and artifacts were pillaged at this time. In addition, many Korean artisans, particularly potters, were forcibly taken to Japan, which sparked the Japanese ceramic industry.

Korean patriots put up spirited resistance, and thanks to heroes like Admiral Yi Sun-shin (see p. 27), they were able to cut off the Japanese supply lines. The Japanese began to withdraw with the death of Hideyoshi and the war ended at last in 1598, having left a disastrous impact upon Korea.

Korea was again invaded in 1627 and 1636 by the Manchus, who

Admiral Yi Sun-shin
(1545 - 1598)

"He who risks death shall live, and he who seeks life shall die. -Yi Sun-shin

In the annals of naval history, Yi Sun-shin stands out as one of the greatest commanders of all time. Most would agree he is probably the greatest hero Korea has produced.

He entered the military at 31 and from early on demonstrated the characteristics that made him great, effecting innovations in military strategy to fit the situation.

Having served with distinction in numerous minor posts, he was appointed Commander of the Chŏlla-do Left Naval Station at Chwasuyŏng (modern Yŏsu) in 1591. He immediately and energetically set about building up the naval defenses of the area, repairing weapons, building warships and training their crews. He had the famous kŏbuksŏn, or "turtle ships," built on the model of a 15th century ship with added firepower and speed.

These are believed to be the world's first ironclads. Plated with iron, they were covered with numerous spikes which were concealed with mats during battle, which made enemy boarding more treacherous. The bow of the boat was fitted with a dragon's head and in the mouth cannons were also positioned. Additionally, sulfuric fumes poured out of the mouth creating a smoke screen, making it difficult for the enemy to determine the exact location of the ship. Cannons were placed all around, and there were many ports for archers. The turtle ships protected the sailors from arrow and musket fire, and were extremely difficult to board. They were also quick and easily maneuverable.

In the fourth lunar month of 1592, Japan invaded an unprepared Korea and quickly reached Seoul. The royal court was forced to flee. At this point, Admiral Yi fought a series of major naval battles in swift succession. Despite being greatly outnumbered, he won them all and nearly destroyed the Japanese fleet.

On the 18th day of the 11th lunar month, 500 Japanese ships gathered in the strait of Noryang in preparation to go home. Reinforced by the Ming Chinese fleet, the Koreans attacked the retreating Japanese. At the height of the battle, Admiral Yi was struck down by a stray enemy bullet. Calling his son and nephew, who served under him, to his side, he said, "Do not weep, do not announce my death. Beat the drum, blow the trumpet, wave the flag for advance. We are still fighting; finish the enemy to the last one". More than 200 Japanese ships were sunk in that battle.

Koreans are proud of Yi Sun-shin not only because he was a great naval commander and military strategist, but also because he was a man of upright character and unquestionable loyalty to the nation despite personal hardship and unwarranted disgrace. Yi insisted that the only way to save one's life was to risk it. In his honor, he was given a number of posthumous titles, one of which included Ch'ungmugong, or Lord of Loyal Valor, given by King Injo (r. 1623-1649) in 1643.

eventually conquered the Ming in China and established the Ch'ing Dynasty (1644-1911). Around this time, a movement known as the *Shirhak*

Kŏbuksŏn (turtle ship)

School or School of Practical Learning began to gain considerable momentum among liberal-minded scholar-officials as a way to build a modern nation state. They strongly recommended agricultural and industrial modernization, and sweeping reforms in land distribution. Unfortunately, these intellectuals were not in power, and the conservative government failed to incorporate these ideas.

Thus Korea remained a "hermit kingdom" adamantly opposed to opening to the West. Subsequently, Korea was ill-prepared to deal with the rapid change of events at the turn of the century when Japan defeated China, Korea's patron. Japan, which had risen as a new industrial power in Asia, annexed Korea in 1905, and made it into a Japanese colony in

Did You Know? Yi Sun-shin was a man of many talents, one of which was his literary ability. Despite being a military man, he showed surprising style and eloquence in his diaries and his poetry. Here is an example of one of his shijo or poems:

In the moonlight on
Hansan Isle
all alone in my lookout,
I grasp my great sword
at my side
lost in troubled thought.
From nowhere, the wail
of a flute pierces my heart.

(Translated by Han Nae-bok and Elizabeth Lee)

1910, thereby ending the Chosŏn Dynasty.

The Japanese Occupation and Korea's Independence Movement

Japan's government-general in Seoul was mainly interested in economic exploitation, and Japanese farmers and fishermen were given Korean land free or at low cost. Large quantities of rice were exported to Japan, and Koreans faced a serious food shortage. The Korean standard of living deteriorated drastically; hundreds of thousands of Korean farmers were forced to move to Manchuria or Japan, only to find life no easier there.

Colonial rule stimulated the growth of nationalism among Koreans. On March 1, 1919, thirty-three patriots gathered in Pagoda Park in Seoul to proclaim a Declaration of Independence. This touched off a nationwide

In a threatening move in 1907, the Japanese army, demanding the abdication of Chosŏn King Kojong (r. 1863-1907), deployed their artillery on Namsan mountain in the southern outskirts of the capital. Japan eventually colonized Korea in 1910.

An Chung-gŭn (1879-1910),
an independence fighter

movement to demand an end to Japanese colonial rule, which was sadly crushed by Japanese forces, with thousands sacrificing their lives.

This event, later known as the Samil (March 1st) Independence Movement, was a milestone in Korea's fight for independence. Even though it failed to expel the Japanese, it contributed to strengthening the Korean people's sense of national identity and patriotism, and led to the establishment of the Provisional Government in Shanghai and to an organized armed struggle against the Japanese colonialists in Manchuria.

Yu Kwan-sun (1902-1920), a patriot

Japan implemented a policy to assimilate Koreans into Japanese culture. The Japanese language was used in Korean schools, and Koreans were forced to adopt Japanese-style names. Nonetheless, the Korean people

Yun Pong-kil (1908-1932),
an independence fighter

30

managed to retain their cultural identity. Also during this period, many national treasures and cultural artifacts were taken to Japan and have yet to be returned.

The Founding of the Republic

On August 15, 1945, Japan unconditionally surrendered to the Allied Powers shortly after atomic bombs were dropped on Hiroshima and Nagasaki. As a result, Korea was finally liberated, regaining its independence after 35 years of colonial rule. The Korean people were overjoyed, but this joy was shortlived.

Soviet forces quickly occupied the northern part of the Peninsula, while U.S. forces moved into the southern part, under an accord reached at the Potsdam Conference in July 1945. Ideological conflict broke out, and the people were divided over who should rule.

On May 10, 1948, general elections were held in the South, and on August 15, the *Taehan Min-guk*, or the Republic of Korea(ROK), was officially established with Seoul as its capital and Syngman Rhee as the first President. Almost concurrently, a Communist regime was established in the North with Kim Il-sung as the ruler with virtually absolute power. On September 9, 1948, the *Chosŏn Minjujuui Inmin Konghwaguk*, or the Democratic People's Republic of Korea (DPRK), was officially established in the North, with Pyongyang as its capital.

On June 25, 1950, North Korea launched an unprovoked full-scale invasion of the South. After initial success, the N.K. forces were repulsed by combined U.N. forces, and pushed back to the Amnokkang River. The People's Republic of China then intervened and soon the two sides were at a stalemate near the 38th parallel. A ceasefire agreement was signed on July 27, 1953, ending the fighting.

During the three years of war, the entire land was devastated, and the economy was wrecked. Millions of people were left homeless and separated from their families. The damage went far beyond that, though, as this war where Korean fought against Korean hardened the division between the North and South and left scars which still last today.

South Korean soldiers recapturing Seoul in September 1950

After the war, the country faced many problems. Syngman Rhee became increasingly autocratic, and by the late 1950s, he dominated Korean politics. Demonstrations broke out in protest, and on April 19, 1960, students led a popular uprising later known as the Sa-il-gu (April 19) Revolution, which forced Rhee to step down.

The Constitution was amended and in August 1960, Yun Po-sun was sworn in as the President of the Second Republic, with Chang Myon as Prime Minister. However, this was shortlived because on May 16, 1961, a military coup led by General Park Chung Hee took control of the government. He was later elected President. Under his leadership, rapid economic development began.

In 1972, Park had the Constitution revised again under the *Yushin* (Revitalizing Reforms) system, inaugurating the Fourth Republic. The Yushin system gave Park even more power and allowed him to stay in power virtually indefinitely.

Discontent with political repression and economic injustices led to his demise. Park was assassinated on October 26, 1979, and Prime Minister Choi Kyu-hah became acting president. However, his rule was extremely brief. On December 12, 1979, General Chun Doo Hwan came into power in a coup-like military revolt, and was later elected President on August 27, 1980.

In May of 1980, a pro-democracy uprising arose in the southern city of Kwangju, which was later known as the "Kwangju Democratization Movement." Many who were protesting Chun's autocratic ways and fighting for democracy were killed or wounded by army troops sent to suppress them.

The brutality outraged the public. By the mid-1980s, a broad-based mass movement of students, workers, opposition politicians, homemakers and other concerned citizens had coalesced in protest against Chun. Their active calls for direct presidential elections and democracy could not be ignored.

On June 29, 1987, the head of the ruling Democratic Justice Party (DJP), Roh Tae Woo, issued the June 29 Declaration of Political Reforms, which provided for the first direct election of the President in 16 years. However, dissension between opposition leaders split the opposition vote, and Roh Tae Woo was elected President of the Sixth Republic.

A number of measures were taken to lessen the authoritarian nature of the government. Around this time (September 17-October 2, 1988), the 24th Olympiad was held in Seoul. Korea's successful staging of the largest Olympics up until that time signaled the Republic's emergence as a major player on the world stage.

On February 25, 1993, the Kim Young Sam Administration was inaugurated, marking the first time in more than 30 years that the Republic had a President without a military background.

Kim Dae-jung was elected President in December 1997 and inaugurated on February 25, 1998. His "Government of the People" was created through the first ever peaceful transfer of power between the ruling and an opposition party in the 50 years of modern Korean political history.

Reunification remains the long-cherished but elusive goal of all Koreans. Some apparent progress has been made in recent years, but obstacles still linger, and it remains to be seen when Korea will be unified.

Culture and the Arts

Over the course of thousands of years, Korea has developed an incredibly rich variety of cultural and artistic expression. In addition, it has blended foreign influences, especially Chinese, with indigenous elements to create unique beliefs, ways of living, literature and handicrafts. In more modern times, Western influences have been added to the mixture to create a sometimes heart-stopping blend of old and new, and contrasts and juxtapositions in the texture of Korean life.

Traditional Crafts

One branch of Korean arts that directly grew out of the needs of Korean lifestyles is Korean handicrafts, many of which are still produced in Korea much as they have been for hundreds or thousands of years, though now for a slightly different market. Thanks to their quality of workmanship and elegance of design, Korean handicrafts today become prized objects fresh from the maker's hands.

Korean woodwork and lacquerwork, which are among Korea's best known crafts, owe many of their particular qualities to the organization of traditional Korean living spaces. Koreans usually slept and sat on the floor (which Koreans still do in large part: almost any Korean can sit on the floor comfortably for hours without her or his legs falling asleep). Old Korean furniture made of wood emphasized an economic use of space and a simple yet appealing design. Particularly, only the best woods were used and pieces were connected through joining or framing, avoiding the use of glue or nails whenever possible. Accordingly, opaque paint was seldom used in finishing them; rather, the wood was rubbed with oil or painted with transparent lacquer.

Articles of wooden furniture from the Chosŏn Dynasty (1392-1910) include wardrobes, chests, shelves, tables large and small, bookcases, cupboards, and other articles of daily life. Metal ornaments like hinges and locks were made of white bronze (a copper alloy with a large proportion of tin), bronze, copper, and especially iron stained with oil.

But what is really spectacular is the ornamentation of Korean wooden articles using the mother-of-pearl inlay technique, a separate art itself which dates back as far as the Shilla Kingdom (57 B.C.-A.D. 668). In this technique, tiny pieces of eggshell-thin mother-of-pearl

are hand cut into shapes, and then glued into position on the unfinished wood. Then the deep, dark, shiny lacquer, usually black or deep red, is applied, surrounding the intricate designs in shimmering mother-of-pearl. This technique reached its high point during the Koryŏ period (935-1392). Later, in the Chosŏn Dynasty, designs became less delicate and formal, and instead, bolder and more realistic.

Another branch of Korean crafts that has a history of thousands of years is metal-

crafts. A highly sophisticated level of metalcraft skill can be found in a wide range of objects made of gold, silver, bronze, and iron dating as far back as the Three Kingdoms period. In fact, personal decorative pieces were at their finest during the Unified Shilla period (668-935), rather than the later periods. Exquisite jewelry like earrings and bracelets were made of gold and finished with filigree or spangles, and belts entirely made of gold were decorated with hanging jade pendants shaped like commas to oscillate with the slightest motion.

With the introduction of Buddhism,

A Shilla golden crown
(National Treasure No. 87) (left)
Longevity motifs on a chest (above)

Did You Know? Printing in Korea has one of the longest and most brilliant histories in the world.

Movable metal printing typeface was used in Korea as early as 1234, predating the Gutenberg printing press by more than 200 years.

The earliest verified example of movable-type printing is a collection of Zen Buddhist sermons, printed in 1377 during the Koryŏ period. A copy of this edition is currently preserved at the French national library in Paris.

The Emille Bell, the largest Korean bell, dates back to the late 8th century.

the production of Buddhist objects in bronze also flourished during the Shilla period. These included incense burners, gongs, implements, and notably, caskets or cases to contain *sarira*, the ashes of a monk cremated after death. Meant to enshrine the "spritual body," these caskets often took the form of pagodas.

Bronze temple bells were also cast in great quantity but these were not mere sleigh bells. The smallest ones were no more than a foot high, but some were even several meters tall. "Rung" by being struck with a thick piece of wood hanging from the ceiling by a chain, the bell emits a long and penetrating tone. Unequaled in their shape, design, and sound, these bells represent the best of Korean metal art. Tradition has it that the 11-foot Emille Bell, which was cast in 771 and can be heard for forty miles on a clear night, owes its beautiful tone to the crying of a baby sacrificed for the recasting of the bell.

Many Korean crafts continue to be taught to new generations, especially through the "human cultural treasures" whose skills are regarded by the Korean government as part of the national heritage, and who receive government protection and support as such. Although some crafts may no longer be essential to the daily existence of average Koreans', most continue to be readily accessible and to influence the look of Korean lifestyles.

Hanbok
Korean Traditional Dress

The most accessible form of Korean art can be seen on the street and even on Paris runways. The traditional Korean dress, called *hanbok,* are custom-made of various materials and colors according to the age of the wearer and the occasion. Young girls wear bright red skirts (*ch'ima*) and yellow jackets (*chŏgori*) with striped multi-colored sleeves but wear red skirts and green jackets after they get married. Older women choose from a wide variety of bright colors and patterns in fabric. Special, more ornate *hanbok* are worn for special ceremonies. For both men and women, *hanbok* are made of silk brocade or satin for winter, and lighter silks for warmer seasons. For summer, hand-woven ramie cloth is often used, and made into stiffly starched, gauzy outfits.

Under the influence of fashions from T'ang China, Korean noblemen wore big trousers and belted jackets, and noblewomen, long skirt-trousers and hip-length jackets towards the end of the Three Kingdoms period. Later, under Mongol influence, the women's jacket was shortened and the skirt worn high up on the waist. Then, towards the 15th century, the skirt was raised again to be tied high up, just under the arms, and the jacket was shortened pretty much as women's *hanbok* are worn today.

The curved sleeves, the narrow white collar, and the one-sided bow of the woman's *hanbok,* are the three points on which the beauty of a *hanbok* is judged.

The outfit is not complete without accessories. Aristocratic women of the Chosŏn period often spent hundreds of hours embroidering long, heavily ornamented hair ribbons, silk pockets or purses (*pokjumŏni*) for men and women, and *norigae. Norigae* are pendants fastened under the bow of the jacket, that have an ornament, like a jade carving or a small silver knife, with a loop on top and a long silk tassel.

Men's accessories consist mostly of stiff

horsehair hats (*kat*), which were worn pretty much from the Shilla period until early this century, and a long silk cord tied around the chest. But, these days, those accessories are hardly ever worn by men, except on ceremonial occasions.

In fact, traditional clothing is now usually reserved for special occasions, such as weddings, or New Year's, or a 60th year birthday party. Still, on the street or in the subway, you can see people wearing traditional clothing almost everyday, especially older people, who tend to wear *hanbok* more often. Nowadays, more people are wearing modified *hanbok*, which are lose, comfortable and easy to care for.

Pottery

A form of Korean handicrafts that has become one of its most highly developed fine arts, ceramic arts have historically possessed artistry of worldwide fame. It seems that for as long as Korean people have been around, they have made pottery, leaving behind earthenware dated as early as 3000 B.C. After the Shilla unification in A.D. 668, Korean potters began to glaze their pieces for the first time, usually in yellow or green glazes. These pieces included urns, bowls, cups, and jars, which were sometimes decorated with stamped designs or ink drawings, and even roof tiles,

Koryŏ celadon with inlaid designs (12th century).

which were decorated in bas-relief. It was during this period that the celadon glaze for which Korea is so famous began to develop.

Celadon is the name for the clear, delicate, (usually) blue-green glaze which was refined and developed through to the Koryŏ period, when celadon pottery reached its peak. Dishes, cups, vases, bowls, pitchers, and water droppers (used to add water to ink for writing) were the most common forms, made with a subtlety and warmth of line unsurpassed. Techniques of decoration under the glaze were also developed, including the inlay technique, which began during the 12th century.

Other techniques also developed, like carving designs into the clay, reverse inlay (painting the whole piece with different-colored clay, usually white, and scraping it away in designs to the clay underneath), or painting

Punch'ŏng porcelain

designs on the clay with iron underglazes, which would turn black during firing, or copper underglazes, which would turn red, brown, or green.

But the celadon which was so popular during Koryŏ gradually gave way to *punch'ŏng* and white porcelain during the Chosŏn Dynasty. In contrast to the elegance and delicacy of ornamentation on celadon pieces, *punch'ŏng* pieces, loosely brushed with white liquid clay, had a freer, more spontaneous charm. These were decorated with stamped or carved designs underneath the white, or painted with iron glaze on top. The Japanese liked these *punch'ŏng* pieces so much, they kidnapped Korean potters in the 16th century to make them in Japan!

Later, Korean potters began to decorate the white porcelain with iron or copper glaze. Painting the pieces with cobalt blue, which had been introduced in the 15th century, was revived with greater success. These blue-and-white pieces, in the form of jars, bowls, dishes, brush-stands, and water-droppers, favored fresh, clear designs and paintings.

Today, ceramic arts in Korea are continually being developed by new artists who show and sell their work in numerous galleries and stores, just as artists working in other media do.

Did You Know? In a 1994 auction held by Christie's, one of the world's largest and most reputable art auctioneers, a blue-and-white Chosŏn platter was sold for US$3.08 million. It was the highest price ever paid for a Korean ceramic piece.

Calligraphy:
The Art of the Scholar

Writing things down with pen (or pencil) and paper as we do everyday usually doesn't require much effort or thought. Most of us don't worry about our handwriting as long as it's readable. But even calligraphers who write in Romance, Germanic, or Slavic languages, who specialize in producing handwriting that looks a certain way, do not have to face all the iron discipline, as well as dazzling freedom, offered by the art of calligraphy in Korea.

Traditionally, the language of calligraphy in Korea as well as in Japan has been Chinese, the only written language of East Asia for thousands of years. Even after the invention of the Korean alphabet *han-gŭl* in 1446, Chinese continued to be used as the written language of the official sphere until the late 19th century. Because Chinese is written with tens of thousands of characters, each with a different arrangement, number of strokes, and meaning, knowing how to read and write these characters was no trivial task. It was the mark of nobility, for one, because only those who did not have to work could afford to spend their lives practicing and studying these characters; it was also the mark of true learning. In addition, the way in which they were written showed just what kind of scholar, what kind of artist, and what kind of person you were, from the time that Chinese calligraphy was introduced in Korea, about 1,500 years ago.

To do *putgŭlshi*, or brush-writing, as it is called in Korean, you need the "Four Friends of the Scholar." They are the ink, the ink stone, the brush, and the paper, all of the finest quality possible. The ink is made of carbon

43

mixed with glue and fragrance formed into very hard, dense, black blocks. The ink stone is made of stone (usually blue stone) of just the right softness/hardness, with a sloping smooth surface in a depression that holds water at the deep end.

Most important in *putgŭlshi* is the balance of spacing and the proportions of the characters, spontaneously executed with NO retouching. (This is the kind of ink you can't erase with ANY-THING.) You may choose to follow the style of a particular school or tradition, each of which has its own set of rules and aesthetics, based on the artistry of a calligrapher of historical skill.

Starting from the Koryŏ Dynasty, Korean kings adopted the Chinese practice of choosing public officials through a periodic civil service examination. The applicants were tested on their knowledge of Chinese classics and the quality of their calligraphy, among other things. Thus, historically, to attain the highest positions in society depended on how learned a man was and how accomplished his writing style was.

You may have guessed already that *putgŭlshi* is not for the dilettante. Most brush-writing artists today begin with rigorous, long training, and recognized success is for the very few. Even those who learn *putgŭlshi* as amateurs continue to study with their teachers for ten, twenty, thirty years (if they live that long after they start). It is one of the most demanding arts you could choose in Korea, and demands the best of Korean discipline, artistry, and spirituality.

Many of the most accomplished calligraphers were painters too, like Kim Chŏng-hŭi. Using the same brush to create a leaning orchid or wind-blown bamboo grove, these artists might write a poem about what they had painted. Even so, painting in Korea has its own wealth of traditions.

Painting

Koreans, like the people of every country, have painted from the very beginning. The earliest remaining murals are found in tombs of the Koguryŏ Kingdom, dating back to the fourth century. Paintings from this period demonstrate Buddhist influences and already used shading techniques.

The Academy of Painting was established in the beginning of the Koryŏ period. The educated upper-class as well as the professional painters trained at this academy produced works with an increasing diversity of themes in addition to the Buddhist themes of the previous period: portraits, animals, and the "Four Gentleman's Plants (*sagunja*)"— the plumtree, the chrysanthemum, the orchid, and the bambooplant— which represented four different virtues. As with calligraphy, paintings were done with brush and black ink on paper or silk, and so painters

Paintings by Kim Hong-do: Dancer and Musicians (left), Wrestling (right).

 Kim Hong-do
(1745-?)

In the world of Korean painting, there have been many brilliant talents and geniuses,but among the best ranks Kim Hong-do. While his landscapes are considered to be among the best of Korea's realism school and his portraits are also admired, he, along with Shin Yun-bok, are considered to be the flagbearers for the style of genre painting depicting the lives of common people which emerged in the later Chosŏn period. It is for this reason that along with An Kyŏn and Chang Sung-ŏp, he is considered one of the three great masters of the Chosŏn Dynasty.

It is said that when Kim was young, not only was he talented, but also very charismatic, which perhaps added to his style and humor. He was reputed to be very attractive and outgoing, gaining popularity among his contemporaries, and even the king liked him.

When he was 29, he painted the portrait of the crown prince and when he was 44, he traveled around the country and painted pictures of the local scenery, which were then sent to the king. In his 50s, he painted landscapes of mountains, trees and streams from real scenes and created works that were unique in style and technique. Kim had an excellent sense of space, and used swift brush strokes to create strong lines, combining them with soft colors which well represented the emotions of the Korean people .

In his later years he devoted himself to genre painting, the art that depicts scenes from the ordinary events of everyday life. This school of painting was an artistic criticism of the aristocratic *yangban* and its artistic tastes. This may have been somewhat surprising to some, since Kim was a painter employed by the government. His genre paintings included his typically adept depictions of mountains and streams, Taoist immortals, flowers and grasses, but the themes centered on people at work.

His works influenced the styles of many painters to come and left a clear mark on the history of Korean art. His paintings also serve as documentation of the lives of the Korean people during the period.

The paintings that still remain have been designated as national treasures and are exhibited in major art museums throughout the country.

Like many artistic geniuses, Kim Hong-do died lonely, remembered by few, impaired by illness and poverty.

A folk painting, Tiger and Magpie

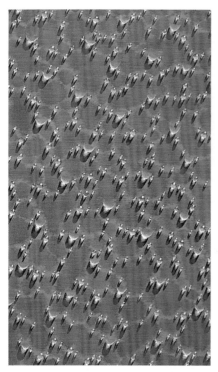

Face by Byon Chong-ha (above)
Water Drops by Kim Tschang-yeul (left)

emphasized line, texture, and proportion to create effects.

Different styles continued to develop through the Chosŏn period, with the introduction of new Chinese styles as well as Western painting techniques. Color was also used in fresh and delicate tints in portraits and tableaux of nobility, usually relaxing, partying.

But the glorious traditions of brush painting went into decline during the 19th and 20th century. An inrush of foreign, modern painting styles entered Korea. And then there was the aftermath of the Korean War.

Disillusioned and hard-pressed, post-war artists threw themselves into the popular aesthetics of French painting of the time, Expressionism. Since then, contemporary painting in Korea has experimented with several schools of modern painting, notably Minimalism. Meanwhile, brush painting continues to both experiment with incorporating these influences and maintaining the age-old traditions.

Sculpture

Unlike paintings made of paper or silk, sculptures from early Korean history, made of stone or metal, were sturdy enough to leave behind ample testimony to the central importance of Buddhism in Korean history and culture. Historically, the best and the most Korean sculpture is Buddhist, or rather, is of the Buddha.

Gilt-bronze Maitreya
(early 7th century)

The first Korean Buddhas of gilt-bronze and clay date back to the sixth century and were found in Koguryŏ. The Paekche and Shilla kingdoms also began to make Buddhas in their own styles shortly after. Buddhas from Koguryŏ had rigid bodies, big hands, big *usnisas* (round bumps on top of the head that symbolize Buddha's supreme wisdom), and barely a smile on their long, thin faces. Buddhas from Paekche, on the other hand, are famous for their benevolent, definitely smiling faces and are warmer, more subtle than the Koguryŏ Buddhas. The Shilla Buddhas had round faces with geometric, stylized features (smiles more subtle than

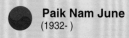

Paik Nam June
(1932-)

How do you look at your television set? Korean video artist Paik Nam June has been asking audiences that question through his work for the past thirty years. Most art critics and artists consider Paik Nam June not only the founder of video art but one of the most important experimental artists of this century.

Much of Paik Nam June's artwork attempts to challenge the way we look at television and relate to it. In one of his first exhibitions in New York City in 1965, he let the audience play with the images on a television screen with giant magnets. Later he used various techniques to distort the broadcast image from famous television shows. His aim was to get his audience to see in a different light the little "sacred" box omnipresent in their homes.

Paik has never hesitated to experiment with "sacred" objects. While studying music in Germany in the 1950s, he performed on pianos which had noise-makers, clocks and assorted household objects glued onto them. Sometimes he would chop or wreck the piano to obtain different sounds. His goal was to use the unexpected to show that art could be spontaneous and engage the audience in a direct manner.

Before moving to America in 1964, Paik helped found the avant garde group Fluxus, which was part of a larger movement to take "art" out of the museum and make it a part of people's everyday lives by experimenting with a variety of different materials and techniques.

Paik Nam June chose to play with video technology. In the 1970s, Paik collaborated with Shuya Abe to build a "video synthesizer" which generated electronic video images timed to music. In its first broadcast in Boston, the video synthesizer played multi-colored images to the music of the Beatles. Excited about video art's possibilities, Paik once proclaimed that the television screen would replace the painter's canvas.

To help make this a reality, Paik moved onto larger, more elaborate projects. After *V-ramid* (1982) and *Tricolor Video* (1982), Paik created the first show broadcast by satellite called *Good Morning Mr. Orwell* (1984), a program which invited performers and artists from around the globe to contribute to what he called a "Global Groove." In commemoration of the 1988 Seoul Olympics, Paik built a massive work entitled *The More the Better,* utilizing over 1,000 video screens of various shapes and sizes.

Born in Korea in 1932, Paik has become a citizen of the world. He was educated in Tokyo and Munich, taught and worked in New York, and his pieces can be found across the globe. This variety in education and living experience has given Paik the luxury of a unique and broad perspective.

Paik Nam June, forever the innovator, has used this global perspective to enhance our perceptions of television, of the world and of each other. Paik Nam June remains active on the international art scene. Though he has already earned his place in history, this dynamic artist has his eyes set securely on the future.

A video art work by Paik Nam June on display at the 1995 Kwangju Biennale.

Paekche's) and realistically sculpted bodies.

Buddha is at his most magnificent in Korea in the Sŏkkuram Grotto, a shrine built during the Unified Shilla period (see Places). Later, during the Koryŏ Kingdom, facial features of Buddha figures became more distinguishably Korean in the eyes and checkbones, but figures were stiff and formal compared to the vitality of sculptures of previous periods. Buddhist sculpture continued to decline with the suppression of Buddhism and the emphasis on Confucianism in the Chosŏn period.

As in all the arts, a new age in Korean sculpture began with the introduction of Western techniques and traditions. Beginning with zealous adherence to academic realism early in the 20th century, Korean sculptors soon branched out into different styles, creating abstract and avant garde works in the 1960s. Many works have an intensely spiritual quality that seems not so removed from Korea's long tradition of Buddhist images. Sculptors in Korea today can choose from a wealth of traditions, new and old.

Architecture

What kind of spaces did ancient Koreans build and live in? Always essential to the construction of all types of buildings in the past was geomancy, the art of determining the place for a structure that would receive the greatest blessing from nature. The most favorable position for a structure was one facing the south, with a mountainous area behind it and a flowing body of water in front. The capital was moved to Seoul in 1394 precisely for these reasons.

The building of temples was stimulated by the introduction of Buddhism via China, and was heavily influenced by Chinese building styles. One of Korea's distinct contributions to East Asian Buddhist architecture was the Korean stone pagoda, of which the Paekche style was dominant during the Three Kingdoms period. Three pagodas stand in a line going east to west, each with its own hall (therefore called the "one-hall per pagoda" style; two-pagoda and three-pagoda structures were also built). Pulguksa, to which Sŏkkuram was built as an annex, is one of the most beautiful of the temples built in the Unified Shilla period (see Places, Kyŏngju).

The woodwork of these temples was often painted in patterns of gorgeous, flaming colors, called *tanchŏng*, a technique still practiced today. Used in traditional motifs and symbols, each color is supposed to have its own meaning: blue=spring, red=summer, white=autumn, black=winter, yellow=the changing of seasons, and reddish brown=harmony.

But of course, people didn't live in these temples. The typical house that Korean farmers lived in, dating back to the Chosŏn Dynasty, was quite different. Always single story, these farmers' homes had thatched roofs and clay walls, and were usually built in an L- or U-shape around an open courtyard.

Did You Know?
Traditional Korean houses have always had central heating. The kitchen stove was connected to vents underneath the floor of the main room (or other rooms), which radiated heat up through the floor. This made it comfortable to sleep and sit on cushions or mattresses on the floor, as Koreans often do. Heated floors, or *ondol*, are still the way in which Korean homes are heated, although now they use pipes heated by gas or electricity instead of firewood.

Music

Even if you've *seen* Korea (at least in the pages of this book), you may not have *heard* her. And how can you know her if you haven't heard her? Unfortunately, this book is not equipped with sound, so you'll have to just read about it here, and go elsewhere to hear, first-hand, an example of Korean music.

Korean music, like Korean art or Korean history, is a category so broad that it is difficult to talk about briefly. Together with more than 60 distinct instruments of which 45 are still played today, Korean music has its own distinct repertory and musical forms. The earliest instrumental music that is still performed today, *Sujech'ŏn*, is a form of court music over a thousand years old, performed by an instrumental ensemble that includes *taegŭm* (transverse bamboo flutes), *piri* (cylindrical oboes), *kaya-gŭm* (twelve-stringed zither), and a variety of drums and other percussion instruments. Court music also included military music and ritual music, which accompanied

A court dance

Confucian rituals or ceremonies at royal shrines. You can listen for yourself at one of two performances of Confucian ritual music held in Seoul every year.

The nobility also enjoyed vocal music in the form of *kagok*, verse sung with a small ensemble in 16- and 10-beat meters, and *shijo*, short lyric songs sung on variations of a basic melody.

More commonly heard these days, however, is traditional music that was for the "common" people: farmers' music, shaman music, Buddhist music, etc. The rhythmic, vibrant music made by farmers is led by the brassy voice of the small gong, the *kkaengwari*, usually to accompany dancing.

Folk songs were commonly based on five- or four-tone systems, unlike the Western twelve-tone system, which means instead of having *do, re, mi, fa, sol, la, ti* (the notes of a major scale), you might have *do, mi, pa, do, ti*. One of the characteristics that distinguishes Korean folk songs is the use of a triple meter, (*one* two three, *one* two three), unlike the double meter (*one* two, *one* two) used in folk songs of Japan and China. Another form of

The Chung Trio: Myung-wha, Kyung-wha and Myung-whun
(1944-), (1948-), (1953-)

Many would agree that the Korean people are musically inclined. Not only does Korea have a rich tradition of music, but the Korean love of music can be seen almost anywhere today. Almost every Korean parent tries to have their children take piano or violin lessons at one point in their lives, creating a huge and sustainable market for small music schools and private tutors.

Singing is even more popular, with normally shy office workers and young women packing into *noraebang* (karaoke rooms) to croon old standards and belt out pop hits. Who among them isn't secretly hoping to be discovered on a Sunday morning variety show or at a college singing competition and make it big?

The Korean passion for music has disseminated overseas: Korean communities abroad sponsor their own song contests, while leading conservatories in America and Europe have a disproportionate number of pupils with the surnames "Kim, Lee, or Park."

The Chung Trio is every Korean mothers' dream come true. They are perhaps the most famous Korean artists ever. They are known as the Chung Trio on the rare occasions when they are able to perform together, but they have also become prominent in their own right as individual musicians. Together they received the Excellence 2000 Award for their contributions in music in the United States and for the first time ever, they were apointed as goodwill ambassadors for the UNDCP in June 1992.

Chung Myung-wha, the eldest of the three, was born in Seoul in 1944. She began piano lessons at the age of four but switched to cello a few years later. At the age of thirteen she received her first musical accolade at a national music competition. Finishing her high school studies at the Seoul Arts School, she went to the Juilliard School of Music in New York, from which she graduated. She went on to study at the University of Southern California. In 1969 she performed at the White House and in 1971, was awarded first prize in the cello division of the Geneva Competition. She has performed with world renowned conductors such as Zubin Mehta and Carlo Maria Guilini.

vocal music of folk origin is *p'ansori,* a musical and dramatic form. Alternately spoken, sung, and acted, a *p'ansori* performance tells one of five basic stories based on old Korean legends, the performer improvising his/her own touches.

Traditional instruments like the *changgo* (hourglass drum) and the *kkaengwari* have gained popularity, and these days it's fairly easy to find cultural centers or private institutions that teach these instruments to amateurs, especially the young.

However, traditional music is not the music of choice for all young Korean people, or even most older Korean people. Classical Western music has long been established and accepted in Korea, and that's what most Korean kids learn: generally, piano for girls and violin for boys, but also just every other instrument you can think of. The first symphony

Kyung-wha first learned to play the piano at the age of 4 and the violin at the age of 6. In 1960 she played in Japan as a member of a goodwill delegation, and in 1961 enrolled at the Juilliard School of Music, where she studied under virtuoso Ivan Galamian. In 1965 she was the second musician from Asia to perform at the Miami Concert Hall. Her accolades include first place in the New York Leventritt Music Competition in 1967. She has given over 100 performances with such world-class orchestras as the New York Philharmonic and the London Symphony and with prominent conductors like Andre Previn and Leopold Stokowski.

Myung-whun also began playing the piano at the age of four and by the time he was seven, he was playing with the Seoul City Orchestra and with the Seattle Orchestra at the age of eight. A graduate of the Juilliard School of Music and Mannes School of Music, he first established himself on the international music scene as a pianist, winning second prize in the Tchaikovsky Piano Competition in 1974. After completing studies in conducting at Juilliard, he made his mark as a conductor and in 1978, became the assistant conductor for the Los Angeles Philharmonic Orchestra. In 1983, he moved to Europe and began conducting Germany's Saarland Radio Orchestra in 1986, and Italy's Florence Opera in 1987. He has also guest-conducted some of the world's most prestigious orchestras: the Berlin Philharmonic, the New York Philharmonic and the Royal Philharmonic, to name a few. In recognition of his talents, he was appointed the musical director and conductor for the Bastille Opera House in Paris in 1989. Chung was also awarded the 1989 Arturo Toscanini prize for conducting.

Although Chung is credited with turning around the struggling Bastille, he was unceremoniously sacked in 1994 after a change in management. Chung and Hugues Gall, the new administrator, locked horns over Chung's refusal to renegotiate his contract over artistic control, pay, and terms of service. After a lengthy court battle, Chung agreed to step down after the first performance of the 1994 fall season.

He is now the music director for the Santa Cecilia Orchestra in Rome and occasionally works with other orchestras as guest conductor.

orchestra, the Korea Philharmonic Orchestra, was established in 1945, and since then Korea has produced a remarkable number of world-class classical musicians, like the Chung trio (see above), cellist Chang Hanna, violinist Sarah Chang, and singers Hans Choi and Jo Sumi among countless others.

But most radio stations today play pop music, which is cranked out by new groups that spring up everyday. From reggae to heavy metal, from smooth Lionel Richie sound-alikes to rap (in Korean!), almost every kind of popular music has been recorded by Korean pop artists, making their own mixes as they gain greater familiarity with borrowed idioms. Whatever music Koreans listen to, almost any Korean would agree that she or he lives in a country of musical people.

Dance

A court dance

From the earliest music to the pounding beat of night clubs, dance usually goes hand in hand with music. Also, like Korean music, Korean dance comes in a wide and contrasting range of styles and origins.

Most movement that accompanies Confucian ritual forms is minimal and stately; sixty-four dancers (men) in eight rows bow slowly in accompaniment to the music during the Confucian ritual ceremony performed today.

The performance of the ancestral ritual in honor of the 20 or so rulers of the Chosŏn Dynasty involves a wider range of movement, and the dancers (again, eight rows of eight men), dressed in rich purple robes, circle their arms and lift their feet from the ground, in addition to the reverential bows.

Court dance developed more freely under Buddhism, than under Confucianism. During the Koryŏ period, elaborate court dances were performed by women, with stage properties and magnificent costumes. Dances were also performed to ask Buddha to let

Sŭngmu (monk's dance)

58

Chinju kŏmmu (sword dance)

souls enter into nirvana, including the Butterfly dance performed by female nuns, the Cymbal dance performed by male monks, and the Law Drum Dance performed by a solo dancer. In the legend behind this dance, a young woman of no uncertain charms tries to seduce a monk by dressing in Buddhist robes and giving a compelling performance with two sticks on a drum. The fascination of her drumming is so powerful that he can't resist her in the end.

Most of the costumes worn in court dances cover the entire body, and the legs are hidden under full robes and skirts. Then, what did the audience seek in the dance? Obviously, the emphasis was not on the full, athletic extension of limbs and high jumps. Instead, the beauty of these dances depended on the subtlety of expressive gestures, smooth and uninterrupted movement, and an unceasing, spiritual intensity.

Although a mixture of Buddhist and Confucian influences can be found in most traditional Korean dances, among those that remain today, the most popular belong to the commoner:

T'alch'um (traditional mask dance)

59

Salp'uri (shamanist dance)

shamanist and farmers' dances, in which dancers followed and improvised on basic movements. The shaman, or *mudang*, who was the people's communication link to spirits, performed dance rituals to console the spirits of the dead, ask for good fortune, etc. Whether the hypnotic, unrestrained movement of a shaman ritual or the elegant movement of *salpuri*, shamanistic dance is powerfully rhythmic and so emotionally charged it's impossible to not feel yourself get caught up in it. Many of the shaman-based dances depend on a marvelous dexterity of expression in complex and subtle rhythms.

Many farmers' dances are influenced by Shaman dance. Following the lunar calendar, farmers' dances are usually performed twice a year, vigorous and celebratory. Alternately leaping and flexing deeply close to the ground, dancers follow singing and rhythms played by the *kkaengwarri*. But the most popular dance of folk origin these days is the mask dance or *talch'um*. Both drama and dance, *t'alchum* pokes fun of the nobility in comic scenes with shamans, corrupt monks, thick-headed nobility, quarrelling spouses, and more. Wearing stylized masks that proclaim the identity of the characters, dancers swing through deep plies, leap, and gesture broadly with their heads to help tell the story.

Although these dances once were performed in small villages, most people see them these days in modern performance halls. In keeping with these changes in venue, Korean dancers have continued to master new forms and traditions. Korean dancers began to study abroad early this century, bringing back other techniques when they came home. The first ballet company was formed in the late 1940's Korean liberation from Japan and balletic technique continues to be a strong basis for most Korean dancers today. Modern dance schools have also established themselves in Korea, beginning with the Martha Graham technique. Interestingly enough, the newest and most powerful trends in Korean modern dance performance these days blend new styles with traditional dance movement, continually creating innovative movement that is uniquely Korean.

Fan Dance

Places

For such a small land, Korea is packed with fascinating geographical features and places of historical interest and legend. Korea even has its share of natural wonders which defy rational explanation.

Although the survey below is sketchy, we hope that you will get an idea of the rugged terrain of land and history that characterizes Korea.

Mount Sŏraksan

Long overshadowed the Kŭmgangsan mountains in North Korea, Mt. Soraksan is nevertheless quite stuning in their own right all year round. One look and you'll understand why it's the stuff of legends.

Other mountains in Korea may be higher, but none can boast of Mt. Sŏraksan magnificent range of rock formations, ravines, valleys, lakes and waterfalls.

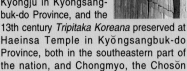
Some of the more interesting things to see include: *Hŭndŭlbawi* or "Rocking Rock," a boulder that can be pushed by anyone without danger of it rolling away; Ch'ŏnbultong Valley, whose stone formations look uncannily like humans and animals; and Taesŭng Waterfall, where a mountain spirit was said to have taken refuge from an attacking monster, which was killed by a heavenly lightning bolt.

The 354 km^2 (136 mi^2) national park is also home to several Buddhist temples and hermitages, the most famous being Shinhŭngsa temple. There are also some modern ski resorts.

Huwon and Ch'angdŏkkung

You can take your pick of Seoul's four Chosŏn Dynasty palaces, all within walking distance of each other, but the personal favorite of many is Ch'angdŏkkung. Ch'angdŏkkung is the best preserved of the palaces, but also the most poignant and accessible.

The palace was constructed in 1405 by King T'aejong as an annex to Kyŏngbokkung Palace and enlarged continously. But everything was

Ch'angdŏkkung Palace

destroyed by fire in the Hideyoshi invasion of 1592. Though the palace was reconstructed during the reigns of King Sŏnjo (r. 1567-1608) and Kwanghaegun (r. 1608-23), most of the structures were destroyed again in the coup that overthrew Kwanghaegun in 1623, and were rebuilt by 1646. Unfortunately, this was not to be the last fire, but Ch'angdŏkkung nevertheless served as the royal residence for Yi kings and queens from 1611 to 1872. The royal family returned to Ch'angdŏkkung in 1907.

Until 1989 the palace was the residence of the last surviving member of the royal family, Princess Yi Pang-ja, who was the wife of Chosŏn's last crown prince, Yi Un. She lived until the age of 87, a firsthand witness and humble survivor of the turbulences of modern Korean history.

Another feature that distinguishes Ch'angdŏkkung from the others are the royal garages which still house the first car in Korea, a Cadillac introduced in 1903 by its proud owner, King Sunjong.

But Ch'angdŏkkung's biggest attraction is *Huwon*—the Back Garden. *Huwon* did not escape the ravages of the Japanese invasion of 1592, but most of the original buildings were rebuilt by King Injo (r. 1623-48) and his successors. Members of the royal family relaxed and held parties on its 32-

Kyŏngbokkung was the largest (500 buildings in its prime) and the most significant historically (Ch'angdŏkkung was built as its adjunct). According to geomancers,the building was demolished in 1997. The Japanese built their administrative building, right in the middle of the palace grounds to obstruct the flow of *ki* (energy).

Ch'anggyŏnggung was a Koryŏ Dynasty summer palace and thus it lies on an east-west orientation, rather than the Chosŏn Dynasty's north-south layout. The palace also housed a zoo, which has since been relocated to Seoul Grand Park.

Tŏksugung Palace is rather an anomaly. Situated right across from City Hall, it was the last of the royal palaces built, and served as temporary lodgings twice in its history. A Renaissance-style building on its grounds serves as a modern art museum, and nowadays as the back-drop to wedding photo shoots.

Huwon (Back Garden), Ch'angdŏkkung Palace

hectare grounds. Huwon's landscaped gardens, woods, ponds and pavilions exemplify the principle of harmony with nature that underlies the beauty of Korea's traditional gardens.

Mt. Maisan and Towers

Near Chŏnju in Chŏllabuk- do province you may come across a strange sight, a mountain that forks apart in mid-air. Locals will tell you that the slightly taller half of "Horse Ear Mountain" is the husband.

Legend has it that two mountain spirits ascending to heaven had to make their climb before dawn to avoid being seen by humans. Up they scurried until the wife felt a prickly sensation. A diligent housewife who had come out to draw some water spied them, and the wife told her husband to stop. But he ignored her and climbed even faster. As punishment for being seen, they were frozen into rock right at the moment he turned his back on her in disgust.

Mt. Maisan is also famous for a series of stone towers or pagodas which were singlehandedly built by an eccentric hermit named Yi Kapryong some 100 years ago. Like the pyramids of Egypt, these towers, numbering more than 80, are engineering marvels. Working only at night for more than ten years, Yi would place natural stones layer upon layer, without the use of any mechanical tool or mortar. The tallest ones stand over 10 meters high, but they are in no danger of falling despite the absence of mortar. They have withstood the ravages of time for more than a century, even typhoons which uprooted huge trees.

Stone towers on Mt. Maisan

How did he do it and why? To his daughter-in-law's query he replied that he did not do them alone; a heavenly spirit descended to earth every night and helped him with its mighty strength. The pagodas were intended for the salvation of all humankind. To strengthen their spirit, he brought stones from celebrated mountains and rivers from all over the country and included some in each tower. While he worked on these pagodas, he lived on a diet of only pine needles, and he also wrote a Sacred Book before he died at the advanced age of 98. Unfortunately, no one yet has been able to figure out the mysterious script he wrote in.

Buddhist followers doing *t'apdori*, a ritual of walking around a pagoda

Shrines

Countless shrines dot the countryside. But they honor not so much the individual heros as the values they lived for and died by. Many are memorials to the faithful daughter or son, for Koreans revered *hyodo-sasang* (filial piety) as the highest virtue.

Some even honor animals. In the village of Osu in Chŏllabuk-do province, you may find a gravestone marked "the grave of the faithful dog." It was erected in honor of a dog who sacrificed his own life while trying to put out flames engulfing his master, who had passed out from drink. The local magistrate himself reportedly wrote the inscription.

69

But the most heartbreaking legend in Korean folklore is the inspiration for Howŏnsa, the Temple of the Tiger's Wish, in Kyŏngju. Tigers feature prominently in Korean folk literature, usually as the affectionate dupes or scheming enemies of humans, but the female tiger of this tale is a noble creature, a rebuke to lesser humans.

According to the story, an ambitious young man named Kim Hyŏ n met a beautiful young woman at the Hŭngnyunsa temple near Kyŏngju during an annual festival in the eighth lunar month. For eight days until the

full moon, the one who walked around the pavilion the most times would have his or her wish granted. Meeting every night in silence, Kim Hyŏn and the woman fell in love.

On the last night, Hyŏn begged to follow her home. He did not understand her reluctance until he reached the house and met her mother—a tiger. Immediately her three brothers came home and sensed his presence. The woman begged them to spare him, agreeing to sacrifice herself as heaven's punishment for her brothers'

excesses.

Hyŏn was horrified. He refused to go along with her plan of making him a hero by slaying her as a tiger. Nevertheless, the next morning a tiger rampaged through the market and Hyŏn was called upon to hunt it down.

Away from the public he could not bring himself to touch a hair of his beloved. Resigned, she changed back into a woman, took his sword, and told him she could not avoid her fate. But if he would only build a temple in her memory then she would surely come back in her next life as a

Two of the four *Sach'ŏnwang*, Guardian kings of the cardinal directions; Buddhist followers practicing *ch'amsŏn*, a Zen meditation.

human, as she had wished for at Hŭngnyungsa. That was the only way they could be together. With that she stabbed herself and died as a tiger.

Kim Hyŏn was shower-ed with honors and riches, fulfilling his own wish. And he built the temple, but although he visited it everyday, nothing could assuage his bitter grief and loss.

Chejudo Island

Chejudo Island off the southern coast is an anomaly in many ways. In the past it served as the place of exile for disgraced officials. Today it is a resort island, the favorite destination of honeymooners and scores of golfers from Japan, inspiring the nickname "Hawaii of the Orient."

It's the largest of the thousands of islands that dot Korea's coastline, with 1,845 square kilometers of extinct volcanos, sparkling beaches and fishing villages. For its natural abundance, Chejudo is also called the "Emerald Isle of the Orient."

Chejudo is located in a semi-tropical belt where crops grow nearly year round. With average temperatures of 24⁰C (6⁰C in winter, and snow on mountain peaks), 1,700 different kinds of plants from semi-tropical to frigid zone species flourish naturally. Chejudo even produces oranges and bananas.

When Koreans think of the Chejudo of the past, they think of three things: wind, rocks, and horses. It is so windy on the island that rocks are incorporated into the local architecture to weigh structures down. And the most popular postcard image of Chejudo is probably of Mt. Hallasan (1950

Tolharubang, Stone Grandfather.

meters) in the background and rape flowers swaying in the wind.

The second most famous image may be the peculiar *tolharubang* ("Stone Grandfather"), sculptures of lava and basalt rock. They look like short totem poles with stylized features—bulging eyes, elongated noses and ears—and serve a similar function in protecting villages.

A legacy of Chejudo's past are horse and cattle ranches. The horses are descendants of Mongolian war-horses raised for Korean armies, while herds of cattle today are bred for beef.

But as an island, Chejudo is better known for its marine products. Seaweed and shellfish, particularly abalone, oysters and octopus, are the major catches of graceful women divers known as *haenyŏ*. Distinctive in their black suits and white headgear, the *haenyŏ* are the traditional breadwinners of Chejudo households. Chejudo is the only place in Korea where you'll find something close to a true matriarchy.

Not only do Chejudo's architecture, climate and family hierarchy differ from the mainland's, but so do its dialect and diet. Islanders speak the same Korean language, but their accent is so thick as to be almost incomprehensible. Their diet is simpler with fewer side dishes and more

Pulguksa Temple

emphasis on seafood. Because of the warmer climate, kimchi is not an essential element of the Chejudo table.

Chejudo's physical attractions are many to be sure, but perhaps it occupies a special place in Korean hearts because although it is only 60 miles away from the mainland, it really is a world apart.

Kyŏngju

In its heyday, Kyŏngju, the capital of the Shilla Kingdom and of the Unified Shilla state later, was one of the world's greatest cities. UNESCO cited Kyŏngju as one of the world's top ten historic sites in 1979, while Koreans justifiably call it the "Museum without Walls" due to a remarkably intact collection of historical buildings, temples, tombs and artifacts and royal burial mounds.

For a thousand years before Shilla defeated neighboring Paekche and

Tabotap and Sŏkkatap pagodas in Pulguksa Temple.

Koguryŏ in A.D. 668 (see "History"), Kyŏngju was a sleepy provincial city. But with hard-won confidence and wealth, products of victories over two more established societies, Kyŏngju began to flourish as a center of the arts and religion as well as politics. A consolidation of the already developed cultures of Paekche and Koguryŏ, close links with the brilliant culture of T'ang China, and the prominence of Buddhism were other factors that helped to form Kyŏngju's golden age. Kyŏngju artisans were especially famed for their masonry and metalcraft.

Unfortunately, Kyŏngju's fortunes began to decline in the 9th century as Shilla lost its luster and strength, finally perishing in A.D. 935. Although it is no longer a major city, Kyŏngju retains its distinction as the single most significant depository of Korea's cultural heritage.

Kyŏngju's most famous landmark is Pulguksa Temple, built in A.D. 535 and enlarged in A.D. 751. Its name, meaning "Land of Happiness," indicates the ebullient confidence of a country that lacked for nothing.

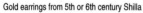

Gold earrings from 5th or 6th century Shilla   Ch'ŏmsŏngdae Observatory

Originally the temple comprised over 80 wooden buildings, but Pulguksa was scaled back in the Koryŏ and Chosŏn Dynasties as anything regarded as a challenge to Confucianism was systematically destroyed. The temple was almost completely ruined by the Hideyoshi invasion during King Sŏnjo's reign in the 16th century. Reconstruction was attempted in bits and pieces but Pulguksa was only restored to a measure of its former glory after its site was completely excavated from 1969 to 1973. All stone structures, however, are original.

Near the Kyŏngju National Park is Ch'ŏmsŏngdae Observatory, the world's first known astronomical tower built sometime between 632 and 647. Apparently its unusual bottle shape is not the result of fancy: researchers believe that the tower was built according to complex mathematic formulae. The 12 stones of the base seem to correspond to the months of the year, and the 30 layers of stone represent the days of the month. The 24 stones that jut out at regular intervals correlate to the 24 seasonal subdivisions of the lunar-solar calendar (see Holidays). In all there are 366 stones, one for each day of the year.

Sŏkkuram grotto (National Treasure No. 24)

The crowning achievement of Buddhist Shilla may be the Sŏkkuram Grotto, a granite-domed feat of engineering housing a seated Shakyamuni facing the East Sea and surrounded by bas-reliefs of bodhisattvas.

It was built as an adjunct to Pulguksa temple by Prime Minister Kim Tae-sŏng under King Kyŏngdŏk in A.D. 751. According to the *Samguk-yusa* (History of the Three Kingdoms) by the monk Iryŏn, more than religious fervor compelled Kim. Sŏkpulsa (or the "Light of Truth"), as it was first called, was a monument to Kim Tae-sŏng's parents.

Kim Tae-sŏng was originally born to a poor family, but an offering at a temple enabled him to be reincarnated as the son of high-ranking Kim Mun-ryang. One day while he was hunting bears on Mt. T'oham, the youth was struck by an epiphany and vowed to build Pulguksa for his parents of this world, and the Sŏkpulsa for his parents of the other world. But it is the rest of us who appreciate the artistry and majesty of the shrine today.

The DMZ and Panmunjŏm

The Demilitarized Zone remains a scar in the consciousness of the Korean people, but it is undeniably fascinating as the last physical vestige of the Cold War, a tense flashpoint for possible hostilities, and an arena for subtle rivalries between South and North Korea. All this only 44 kilometers from Seoul.

Geographically, the DMZ is a four-kilometer-wide strip that stretches 250 kilometers (155 miles) from the east to west coast and is divided in half by the Military Demarcation Line. The zone is supposed to be neutral, but since 1974 UN and South Korean authorities have discovered several tunnels penetrating the southern half, presumably for the transport of

Did You Know? The DMZ has become the favored preserve of otherwise endangered floral and faunal species? Since no one has been allowed to walk around there for more than forty years, a strange twist of fate has made this remnant of past conflict a surprisingly peaceful sanctuary for birds, boars, bears, deer and other species, attracting researchers from all over the world.

North Korean troops. In the tunnels, visitors can witness with painful clarity the backbreaking, yet futile, toil that must have gone into the boring of solid granite.

It's easy to arrange a visit to the DMZ. Tour buses regularly ply Chayuro (Freedom Highway) and cross the Freedom Bridge into the village of Panmunjŏm, the site of armistice negotiations that ended the Korean conflict in 1953. (The two sides are technically still at war; they are merely observing an extended cease-fire.) Panmunjŏm is also the seat of the intermittent dialogue between the Democratic People's Republic of Korea (North Korea) and the Republic of Korea(South Korea).

Sports and Leisure

Sports and leisure have come to play an important part of everyday life for many Koreans, particularly in recent times. Perhaps because of the many difficulties the country has faced, the Korean people have a particularly strong love of sports and recreation. Many people say that Koreans are passionate people: as hard as they work, they love to play even more. At company picnics, you can see an intensity and energy seldom matched in the office place. The younger finally get to show their stuff, while the slowly-aging try to relive their youth, but instead feel their age.

Takkyŏn, a Korean traditional martial art

As Korea continues to develop, athletes at all levels are becoming more and more competitive. Furthermore, since the standard of living has sharply risen, people are finding a wider variety of athletic and recreational activities they can indulge in.

Spectator Sports

Interest in spectator sports has mushroomed in the last several decades. From archery to yachting, Koreans compete both domestically and internationally, doing well in some, and not as well in others. Here is a look at some of the more popular sports.

Baseball

Just as in most places in the world, baseball is one of the most popular sports in Korea. Getting their first glove or bat on their birthday remains an unmatched thrill for young Korean boys, and most have their own favorite slugger or team. Its popularity can be easily seen throughout the country—from children wearing baseball caps or reading baseball comic books to businessmen sitting on the subway reading the sports newspapers to find out the scores and stats.

Baseball was first played in Korea

around 1906. A professional baseball league was inaugurated in 1982 with six teams, with two more teams added later, in 1986 and in 1989. Each team is sponsored by a different Korean corporation and plays a 126-game season.

There are presently eight teams in the league. Foreign players began to play from the 1998 season.

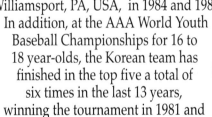

At present, 16 foreign players, from the United States, Venezuela and the Dominican Republic, are playing for the eight teams. The Korean youth teams are also very competitive and have fared particulary well in international competition. Korea has twice won the Little League World Series held annually in Williamsport, PA, USA, in 1984 and 1985.

In addition, at the AAA World Youth Baseball Championships for 16 to 18 year-olds, the Korean team has finished in the top five a total of six times in the last 13 years, winning the tournament in 1981 and more recently in 1994.

Recently, Korean baseball stars have begun to make a name for themselves in overseas leagues. After a rough start in the USA's Major Leagues, Park Chan-ho is now a starting pitcher for the Los Angeles Dodgers. In Japan, Sun Dong-yol and Lee Jong-beom are top players for Japan's Chunichi Dragons.

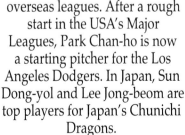

Football (Soccer)

The Korean people by tradition love football. While baseball may be more popular among the young, football is loved by people of all ages. Some like it because it is simple to learn and play and does not require much equipment; others, because to be good requires such an incredible balance of speed, stamina, coordination and awareness; and still others, because they just like to kick things.

Korea was the first country in Asia to field a professional team. The professional league, first established in 1983, changed its name to the Korean League in 1994 and there are 10 teams in the league. Foreign players began to play from the 1996 season. Currently 23 foreign players from Brazil, Ukraine, Russia, Romania and other countries are playing for seven teams. This league has firmly established Korea as a powerhouse in Asian soccer. Korea has won the gold medal at the Asian Games three times and has won the Asian Cup twice. Its youth teams have fared even

better: Korea has been the winner of the Asian Youth Championships (the qualifying tournament for the World Youth Championship of the FIFA/Coca-Cola Cup) a total of seven times and runner-up six times.

Korea has also enjoyed increasing success in the international arena. The Republic of Korea is the only Asian nation to qualify for the World Cup Final Competition five times and has made the last four consecutive finals. In the 1994 World Cup Games, held in the United States, the South Koreans had their best showing ever, registering draws against both Spain and Bolivia, and losing by only a single goal to perennial powerhouse Germany. At the 1998 Finals in France, Korea failed to advance to the second round, despite high expectations, but the team did manage to hold Belgium to a draw. In recognition of its soccer prowess, Korea was chosen to cohost the 2002 World Cup Finals with Japan.

A number of Korean stars have played for foreign pro teams, the most notable probably being Cha Bum-kun, nicknamed "The Panther," who played in the German Bundesliga for almost a decade in the '70s and '80s. Midfielder Kim Joo-sung, once known as the "Little Samson" since he claimed that his strength flowed from his long hair, also played in the Bundesliga.

World Cup

Koreans love soccer—or football as they call it. Children and young adults play in any vacant lot in the summer in much the same way Americans play baseball. Thus Koreans are excited about cohosting the 2002 World Cup Finals—the first in Asia—with Japan and hopes that the championships will put a favorable spotlight on the country in much the same way the 1988 Summer Olympics did.

Ten cities in Korea—including Seoul, Pusan, Taegu and Taejon—will host about half of the game. The opening ceremony will be held in a new main stadium now under

cconstruction in the western outskirts of Seoul. The stadium will hold a crowd of 63,930 fans, including 805 VIPs and 2,024 members of the press.

In addition Koreans hope that close cooperation with Japan in the cohosting of the game will not only make them a great success but will also help heal the wounds of past relations. The 10 Korean host cities are arranging friendly matches with the 10 Japanese host cities in preparation for the games.

South Koreans also hope that North Korea will be able to share in hosting the World Cup Finals. At the request of South Korea, FIFA has said that North Korea will be allowed to host two games. North Korea, however, has yet to respond.

Taekwondo

Taekwondo is a self-defense martial art that has developed in Korea for over 2,000 years. While similar in some ways to Chinese kungfu, Japanese karate, and the other Korean martial arts such as hapkido and tangsudo, taekwondo tends to emphasize the use of the legs and feet through powerful kicks. Taekwondo experts have amazed people throughout the world with their acrobatic skills, breaking boards 10 feet off the ground or hitting multiple targets in mid-air. Taekwondo has become a Korean national sport and is a compulsory course for training in the military. Like other martial arts, taekwondo focuses on the development and discipline of both the body and the mind, one reason it has spread swiftly to many foreign countries. Currently, some 30 million people practice the sport in more than 140 countries.

Taekwondo was adopted as a regular event in the 10th Asian Games, and Korea's athletes demonstrated their dominance by winning seven of eight gold medals. A demonstration sport at the 1988 and the 1992 Summer Olympics, taekwondo will be a medal sport at the 2000 Summer Olympics to be held in Sydney.

Others

There are also other sports which are popular in Korea. Boxing was perhaps the first sport in which Korean was truly internationally competitive, and thus remains quite popular. Kim Ki-su took the World Boxing Association (WBA) junior middleweight title in 1966, and since then, 29 other Korean boxers have become world champions, mostly in the lighter weight classes.

Lately, basketball seems to be the latest craze, especially among the younger generation. It is not uncommon to see groups of kids hanging around the nets after school and on weekends sporting their hi-tops and baggy shorts trying to make everyone else

Did You Know? The strongest man under the heavens is Korean. Actually, that may not be true, but Korean *ssirŭm* fans would like to think so. *Ssirŭm* is a traditional Korean form of wrestling believed to have originated about 1,500 years ago. In a ring of sand seven meters wide, two competitors grab each other by a sash tied around both the waist and upper thigh and try to throw or push the other to the ground. A professional league was formed in 1983 and now wrestlers are divided into weight classes. Eight times a year a national tournament is held and the winner of the unlimited class division is given the title "Strongest Man Under the Heavens."

look bad. The enthusiasm in basketball is seen everywhere: from the professional Korean Basketball League to the start of an annual 3-on-3 tournament at the Han-gang Riverside Park; from the increasing number of basketball shows and comic books on basketball to the explosion of NBA paraphernalia favored by Michael Jordan-wannabe's. College and corporate semi-pro teams already have a lot of fan support, and the top hoopsters are among the most popular celebrities in Korea.

For the more intellectually-

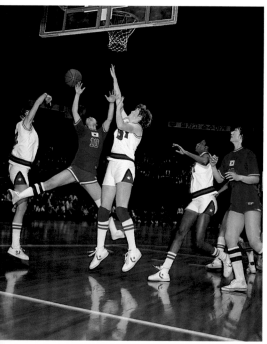

oriented, the name of the game is *paduk*. Also known as *weiqi* in China or *go* in Japan, this game is a traditional Asian board game of military strategy where players try to capture as much territory as possible. Korea has dominated the professional scene in the '90s, and is currently possessor of all four major championships.

Two other military-related sports in which Koreans are now among the world's best include archery and its more modern cousin, shooting. Korean women won the gold medals in the individual and team archery

competitions at the last two Olympics and the men did almost as well. The Korean team also took two gold medals in shooting at the 1992 Barcelona Olympic Games.

Table tennis is another sport in which Korea has medaled well. The Korean teams have taken home a total of eleven medals in table tennis (also known as pingpong) in the last three Olympics, including two golds. Korea has also done well in the World Championships, winning four medals in 1993. Hyun Jung-hwa capture of the women's singles. The women's teams have finished in the top three in every championship since 1985.

Short-track speed skating is the latest sport in which Korea is making its mark. In the 1992 Albertville Winter Games, Korea's Kim Ki hoon won the men's 1,000 meters and anchored the gold medal-winning men's relay, while the women's team took the silver. At the 1994 Lillehammer Games, the men and the women took two golds each. Korea triumphed again in the 1998 Nagano Games with three gold medals in short-track.

Sohn Kee-chung   Hwang Young-cho

The Olympics

The Olympics have always had a special meaning for the Republic of Korea, since it was one of the first international events that the Republic participated in as an independent nation. The Republic first competed in the Olympics in 1948 at the London Olympics. While the Korean team only managed to win two bronzes at that time, South Korea has since then done well for a nation of its size, particularly in the last several Olympics.

When Korea hosted the Olympic Games in Seoul in 1988, it earned its best result, ranking fourth in the gold medal count with 12 and sixth in overall medals with 33. In the 1992 Barcelona Olympics, it placed seventh out of 172 countries, garnering 12 golds, 5 silvers

Did You Know? Korea has a history of great marathon runners. At the 1936 Olympics Sohn Kee-chung and Nam Sung-yong took the gold and the bronze in the men's marathon, surprising most onlookers as Sohn set an Olympic record. Unfortunately, they were forced to run under the Japanese flag.

So Yun-bok followed in winning the prestigious Boston Marathon in 1947, and in 1950, Korean runners swept first, second and third in Boston, led by Ham Ki-yong. This old glory was recaptured when Hwang Young-cho beat the favorites and won the men's marathon gold at the 1992 Barcelona Olympics.

93

and 12 bronzes. In the 1996 Atlanta Games, Korea ranked eighth, with 7 golds, 15 silvers and 5 bronzes.

Recreational Sports

Just as spectator sports have been picking up in Korea, so have recreational sports. As the nation grows richer, people of all ages are finding more time, money and energy to enjoy themselves and stay in shape, and so there are more and more things to do.

Since Korea is about 70 percent mountainous, Koreans have traditionally enjoyed mountain climbing. On the weekends, mountain trails are usually packed with families or hiking clubs spending the day away from the city. Some go for the exercise, even working out at exercise facilities near peaks, while others go to pay their respect at Buddhist temples located high up on some of the mountains, and others go to collect the fresh mountain spring water. However, most just go to relax and breathe the fresh air with their friends.

Modern sports centers where people can swim, bowl, lift, work out, do aerobics, or a number of other things, have popped up throughout the country. Buses truck around the

apartment complexes to pick up little kids learning how to swim and young mothers trying to maintain their pre-marriage figures with aerobics. At the center, they often encounter tired businessmen trying to work off the spare tire around the waist and counter the excesses of last evening's night out on the town in the jacuzzi and sauna, or else young men trying to pump up. At the bowling lanes, a random mix of people roam late into the night. From bored homemakers to businessmen, from young couples in love on an innocent date to groups of lonely hearts of both sexes—they all come in search of strikes.

There are also thousands of places where people can train in not only taekwondo, but hapkido, judo, kemdo, kungfu, or almost any other martial art. Parents like having their children learn such things, not only to make them stronger, but also to help them discipline the mind. More and more females are also taking classes for self-defense. Others like to go simply for the camaraderie or to stay in shape.

The younger generation in Korea is enjoying the recent wave of modernization and Westernization, finding a much wider range of things to do in terms of recreation beyond the usual movie or drinking.

Many health-oriented students form sports clubs on campus or in their neighborhoods. Beyond the usual pick-up games of basketball, soccer, baseball or *chokku* (a kind of foot-volleyball), they often organize trips to go skiing, hiking, and sometimes even hang-gliding.

The more adventurous can go windsurfing and water-skiing, not to mention the universal classic pastime, fishing. More and more swimming pools have been built, but they are usually crowded, as are the beaches. In the city, people can go to batting cages and enclosed driving ranges to brush up on their skills.

Billiards and table tennis have always been popular among college-age students, and particularly in the areas around colleges, it is impossible to walk more than 50 feet without running into one hall or the other. Recently, pocket billiards has become very popular among the hipper crowd, and more and more pool halls and cafes are carrying pocket pool tables.

The older generation, too, seems to be taking greater interest in recreation and fitness. Besides mountain climbing, many enjoy walking or simple games of badminton, setting up nets wherever they can. Overweight businessmen are taking time out of their busy schedule to jog, walk, exerbike, work out or do anything else they can to get in shape. An increasing number of businesses are arranging facilities where employees can exercise during breaks and before and after work.

Lately, the most popular sports for adults seem to be tennis and golf.

There are tennis courts at many apartment complexes or schools, as well as many private clubs, and these days, tennis is so popular that it is almost impossible to get court time at nights and on weekends. Golf is much the same way, as middle-aged Koreans have really taken to this placid and scenic sport. As in many parts of the world, many flock to the private golf courses located outside of the city on weekends to let off stress, to schmooze with boss or clients, or just to improve their handicap (and lie about it later). For the more traditional and purist, the above-mentioned *paduk* and *changgi,* the Korean version of chess, are common ways to relax in the evenings or on weekends.

Ch'ajŏn Nori is played not only for fun, but also to foster village teamwork.

Holidays
and Food

Holidays

Although Koreans work hard, they always appreciate a holiday as a time of rest and reunion. Between the two calendar systems in use in Korea, the year is chockfull of special days, and when you add up the personal birthdays and milestones as well, every month brings something to look forward to.

Lamentably, the pace of modern Korea hardly allows urban citizens to keep up with the traditional feast days that their agrarian ancestors enjoyed. Although the two largest holidays, the Lunar New Year's and Ch'usŏk, have retained many of their traditional trappings, observation of other days has diminished to the eating of a special dish. Koreans old enough to remember, however, fondly recall the pleasure of an entire day off from hard labor to celebrate and feast with the entire community, and to wish for good fortune.

The Lunar Calendar

Since the Three Kingdoms period, farmers followed a calendar based on the revolution of the moon around the earth. A month is 29 or 30 days, and there are twelve months in a year. However, this adds up to 354 days a year, compared to 365 in a solar calendar. The 11-day difference is made up every 33 months in a 30-day leap month called *yundal*. Since it is essentially a repeat of the month before, the leap month is considered a blessed period, free of "unlucky" days. Weddings and other ceremonies are purposely scheduled then. Although the Western calendar was officially adopted in the 19th century, many Koreans still calculate important personal days by the lunar calendar.

The list of lunar holidays below is by no means complete. If you were determined to participate in the countless official and unofficial holidays observed in every corner of the country, you'd have time for nothing else. Each region, each religion, and each village has a unique tradition or folk festival, some completely unknown to the rest of the country. What these special days have in common, though, is their celebration of nature, community and family, not to mention their collective wish for prosperity and luck.

Even today in industralized Korea, families flung across the peninsula gather together at least twice a year (creating massive traffic jams!), usually at the household of the oldest male. All the wives help to prepare the feast while children play, and the men sit around talking business.

Traditional Holidays

New Year's Eve—Last Day of the Year
The superstitions and customs of New Year's Eve have since given way to the greater importance of the following day, but surely it can't hurt to revive them for additional luck.

In the past, women would run to the well at dawn to be the first to draw "lucky water." They also began preparing the feast for the next day, including the rice-cake soup in pheasant broth called *ttŏk-kuk* (see below).

Another useful custom was the settlement of outstanding debts by midnight. The household stayed up well after midnight, with even children fighting not to succumb to sleep lest their eyebrows turned white.

Sŏllal (New Year's Day)—First Day of the First Month
This is one of the two biggest holidays in Korea. Korea actually celebrates the New Year twice. While January 1st and 2nd are official holidays, most families make the cross-country voyage to their hometowns for the Lunar New Year, which falls in late January or early February.

As in the West, this day sends off the past year and ushers in the new. Perhaps nobody appreciates the promise of a new start more than a Korean farmer.

In the weeks preceding this day, friends exchange cards to thank each other for deeds of the past and wish them a happy new year. Nowadays

Sebae, bowing to parents and elders, is an age-old New Year's custom.

church-going Koreans send their Christ-mas greetings as well.

For children, the most popular custom is dressing up in rainbow-colored silk *hanbok* and performing the *sebae* (New Year bow) before all the elders of the family and wishing them *bok* (fortune) for the coming year. In turn, they are rewarded with golden words of advice and pocket money, the amount depending on their age and position in the family. This is one custom that is in no danger of dying out from rapid industriali-zation and urbanization, although its focus has shifted from paying calls of respect on elders to paying young children to be good.

Some of the other games that make this day special, but are losing ground to electronic forms of recreation, are a tug-of-war, kite-flying, see-sawing, and *yut-nori*, a kind of board game played with sticks. (See p. 107).

The tug-of-war is more than a game of sheer strength. Because the ropes are bound in such a way as to symbolize the joining of man and woman, the contest promises fertility and productivity for the winning team, essential for farming and fishing communities.

Kite-flying is not only a sophisticated sport in Korea, but also the medium by which the past year's bad luck and illnesses are released to the

Yut-nori, a kind of board game

heavens. Over seventy different designs are known, including the shield kite, the *paduk* (or "go" in Japanese) board kite, skirt kite, and the stingray kite. The most popular kind is the shield kite, with its distinctive round hole.

The hole acts as a propeller which controls speed and direction. These qualities were necessary for kite battles, in which boys tried to cut each others' kite strings, coated with powdered glass.

Traditionally for girls over seven, the see-saw was their window to the world. New Year's Day used to be the only time of the year that girls could see over the courtyard walls. Nowadays, the see-saw is more a test of rhythm and balance than the social event girls looked forward to all year. Jumping up and downn on the low, flat board is devilishly more difficult than it appears. There is no fulcrum, so the momentum comes entirely from the timing of you and your partner's leaps.

The menu for this day varies from region to region and family to family, but common to every table is *ttŏk-kuk*, a soup of sliced sticks of rice cake in beef or chicken broth (instead of pheasant). Koreans say that eating

Yut-nori

This game is ever-popular with young children during major festivals. Although *yut-nori* is very simple on a basic level, even adults can appreciate the skill and strategy displayed by masters.

For, instead of dice or a spinner, the combination of four sticks determines how far you move on the board. You can set up the board anywhere with chalk or a magic marker. The bigger the board, the better.

The sticks are shaped like small canoes, flat on one side and rounded on the other, with tapered ends. On the bottom (flat) side of one stick is a special mark, called *back-do.* Each team has four chips, either black or white. All four chips of one color must go around the board once for the team to win.

The number of spaces you can move depends on how the sticks land after being tossed. When one stick is up (rounded) and the other three are down, the combination is called *do,* which allows one step forward. Two up and two down is known as *kae,* and you can move two spaces. Three up and one down is *kol,* good for three spaces. If all the

sticks are down (flat), this is known as *yut* and you can advance four spaces. Finally, if all the sticks are up, this is called *mo,* which allows you to move five.

You can move your chips separately, or when one lands on the same space as another you can move them together. You can choose to have all four travel in a pack, but the danger lies in being caught and "eaten" by the other team's chips. Whenever your chip lands on a space occupied by the other team's chip, you can make it to go all the way back to the beginning and you get another turn throwing the sticks. If you get the combination of the *back-do* stick up and the others down, you must move one space backwards.

The board is set up with short cuts. Normally, the chips must move around counter-clockwise. If you land on a special circle, you can take the diagonal short cuts instead, depending on where your opponents lie.

No matter how many people play, each team only has four chips. The captain of each side must coordinate the strategies of avoiding, attacking, and doubling in order to bring all four chips around the most quickly.

Unlike other popular adult games, there is no money exchanged but winners may eat extra rice cakes.

ttŏk-kuk means "eating" another year.

Other dishes are dumplings, *pindaettŏk* (mung-bean pancakes—much more appetizing than they sound), and *sujŏnggwa* (cinnamon tea) or *shikhye,* a rice punch.

Families offer food and drink to ancestors in a memorial ceremony. Although memorial rites are held at other times throughout the year, on this day ancestors are served *ttŏk-kuk* as well.

Strings of lanterns festoon a Buddhist temple on Buddha's Birthday.

Buddha's Birthday (Eighth Day of the Fourth Month)

You can always tell when Buddha's Birthday is coming, even if you don't follow the lunar calendar, by the strings of beautiful paper lotus lanterns that the nation's Buddhists begin to hang up a week before. All the major temples hold day-long ceremonies, to which millions of believers flock to pray for good fortune. Many mothers pray especially for the success of their children in school examinations.

Tano ("Double Five," or Fifth Day of the Fifth Month)

To welcome the beginning of summer, memorial rites for ancestors were observed and then the fun began. Women would wash their hair in water from boiling green lentil-jelly (ch'angp'o) and gather herbs for drying. This was the one day of the year that married women were free to visit their own families. Women also swung on long ropes while men engaged in ssirum, or traditional Korean wrestling (see sports).

In anticipation of the heat, kings sent fans to officials while villages sent fans to Seoul. The royal clinic made cheho-t'ang, a health soup, for the king. The traditional menu also included shad fish soup, steamed carp and cherry punch. Round rice cakes flavored with mugwort and other mountain greens are still served in some households.

If rice-cakes aren't enough to relive the spirit of the past, you can go to Kangnŭng in Kangwon-do province for its famous five-day Tano festival. In fact, the government has officially designated the festival itself as "Important Intangible Cultural Treasure No.13." In addition to the folk games played at other times of the year, the festival includes a Confucian ritual, shaman exorcisms, mask dances, *nong-ak* (see p. 107) and even a circus. After working up a vigorous sweat, merrymakers imbibe powerful liquors brewed especially for the week.

Ch'ilsŏk (Seventh Day of the Seventh Month)

This may be the most romantic day of the calendar. Korean legend has it that the Vega and Altair stars are the celestial reincarnations of two lovers, Kyŏnu (Herdboy) and Chingnyŏ (Weaving Maiden), who meet only once a year.

As the story goes, the daughter of the Heavenly King lived on the eastern side of the heavenly stream, or Milky Way, weaving beautiful patterns every night. Worried that she might be lonely, the king married her to a handsome herdboy tending flocks on the western side. But the two lovers were so caught up in romance that she neglected her weaving. In anger, the king banished her back across the stream. Their sorrow moved the king to allow her to cross the stream once a year on a bridge made of magpies and crows.

Rainfall at night signified their tears of joy, while rain on the following morning meant tears of parting.

Foods for this day were rice-cakes, zucchini pancakes, noodles, and cucumber kimchi.

Women in traditional costume make songp'ŏn, the festive rice cake, on Ch'usŏk, the harvest moon festival.

Ch'usŏk ("Harvest Moon Festival")
Fifteenth Day of the Eight Month

This is Korea's other major holiday, and the most generous in spirit. Also known as *Han-gawi*, it is a day of thanksgiving for a good harvest. As on Lunar New Year's Day, families come home from all across the country to celebrate together.

Families traditionally received new clothes on this day but today they are more likely to dress up in hanbok. Faithfully they pay respects to their ancestors with wine, rice cakes, and newly-harvested fruits and grains like chestnuts, jujubes, persimmons, apples, and Korean pears. The day is not complete without the half-moon shaped rice cakes called *songp'yŏn*.

New Year's Day activities and games are popular at this time of year too, when the weather is incontestably brilliant. No wonder Koreans used to say "The sky is high and the horse is fat."

On Hanshik day, falling in early April, and Ch'usŏk, in the fall,
many Korean families visit the ancestral tombs to pay their respects (above).
Nong-ak, famer's dance and band music (below).

Important Korean Dates

New Year's (January 1) : The first two days of the New Year are generally celebrated. The Western one is catching on as it comes right after Christmas. Everyone appreciates the extra days off.

Sŏl (First Day of the First Month by the Lunar Calendar) : This day, which is also known as Lunar New Year's Day, is observed with family rituals honoring ancestors, special food and traditional games.

Sam-il Day (March First) : Independence Movement Day. The Koreans declared their independence from Japanese colonialists in 1919.

Buddha's Birthday (Eighth Day of the Fourth Month by the Lunar Calendar) : Solemn rituals are held at Buddhist temples, and the day's festivities are climaxed by a lantern parade.

Children's Day (May 5) : On this day, children are the center of attention as their parents shower them with presents and take them on outings.

Parent's Day (May 8) : Combining Mother's and Father's Day, this unofficial holiday is considered by some to be superfluous as Koreans honor their parents everyday.

Teacher's Day (May 14) : Teachers occupy a special place in this Confucian society. Until recently, students were forbidden to walk in the shadow of their teachers, literally.

Constitution Day (July 17) : This national holiday celebrates the establishment

of the first Korean Constitution on July 17, 1948. The Republic of Korea was established about a month later.

Liberation Day (August 15) : Taegŭkki, the Korean flag, fly from nearly every building on this day, which marks the end of Japanese colonial rule in 1945.

Ch'usŏk or Harvest Festival Day (Fifteenth Day of the Eighth Month by the Lunar Calendar) **:** This is one of the great national holidays of the year. On this day a feast is prepared and families hold memorial services at the family grave site. Viewing the full moon is a feature of the evening.

Han-gŭl Day (October 9) : Perhaps the only alphabet to have its own day, Han-gŭl is the crowning achievement of the brilliant King Sejong (see **History** and **Korea in Brief**). Among the many inventions of his court, this scientifically-based phonetic alphabet was the most far-reaching, as it freed the populace from the tyranny of memorizing thousands of Chinese National characters.

National Foundation Day (October 3) : Called Kaech'ŏnjŏl Day, this is the day when Tan-gun founded the first Korean Kingdom. (see the **Tan-gun Myth and History**)

Christmas (December 25) : Christianity took hold in Korea only in the 19th century, so this day has less religious significance. Just as everywhere else, though, it's a good time to exchange greetings and gifts. "Grandfather Santa," as he is called in Korea, is somewhat smaller in build than his Western counterpart.

Food

Long ago, an officer fought an unsuccessful military campaign and lost. Abandoned by even the few survivors, he tried to make his way back home alone. But wounded and weak, he could not go very far in the mountains. After a few days he resigned himself to dying when from far off he saw smoke rising from a shabby structure. Bolstered by hope he limped and crawled the entire distance and finally collapsed at the stoop. The smell of spicy food and strong liquor pierced his fog of delirium and gingerly he sat up. A comely young woman passed by him with a tray of bubbling soup, rice, and a few pickled vegetables. Hardly a feast, but to the officer it was the most glorious sight. "Girl, let me have some food," he croaked. She looked at him sullenly. "This is for a guest already. Anyway, you don't have money." The tantalizing food and her brusqueness were maddening, but he made another try. "Do you know who I am? I'm General Kim. I will not fail to reward you when I return home, I promise. I will pay double the price of that meal." She sniffed. "And I'm supposed to believe you?" Meanwhile the food was getting cold. Desperate and crazed, he made his final offer. "Look at my hair. The topknot is proof that I'm *yangban*. I will make you my wife if you give me that food." Suspiciously she removed his headgear. Indeed, the topknot was proof enough for her. She was poor and of low-birth, but she was no fool. To marry this man would elevate her family's status, and enable her to leave this forsaken mountain pub forever. "Come inside, master, and sit at the table. I will prepare you the finest meal you ever had." For want of food, the officer sold his birthright, not unlike Esau did at roughly the same time half way across the globe.

*   *   *

The easiest and most enjoyable way to enter a new culture is through its food. So you can't name the cabinet members of a given country, but you can instantly name its most famous dish. And though we recognize some associations as stereotypes, they allow us to identify with the people of that community more than any other aspect of culture. Perhaps this is because everyone has certain strongly held associations about food, which are remarkably similar throughout the world.

Well, the typically Korean dish is *kimch'i*, and you would not be wrong if you assumed that most Koreans eat *kimch'i* in one form or another everyday. *Kimch'i* is a general term for a pickled vegetable side dish, made of Chinese cabbage, radish, cucumbers or seafood, and red peppers. Scholars have documented over 170 varieties, but the most common is *kimch'i* made with Chinese cabbage.

Kimch'i is but one of many side dishes that accompany rice. Since all the dishes are presented together on a table, Korean etiquette does not require a specific order in eating. Rather, the focus is on the number of dishes.

Traditionally, the number of dishes indicated the position of both the household and the guest. In the Chosŏn period there were five kinds of settings for everyday meals, never mind feasts. Only the royals could afford and enjoy the 12-course meal. The *yangban* class (aristocrats) were

Kimch'i

Tangy and hot, it's the accent and counterpoint to a traditional meal of rice and soup. But nowadays, kimch'i is turning up in pizzas and burgers, making it a most versatile ingredient, not to mention the test of a good cook. Even bachelors who can hardly cook to survive know how to transform leftover kimch'i and rice into sizzling fried rice or bubbling kimch'i stew.

The process of making kimch'i is an excellent example of how Korean women approach cooking. (To clarify, most men never enter the kitchen, and most women only learn how to cook after marrying, under the tutelage of their mother-in-law.)

Measurements? A handful of this, a pinch of that. Food processors? Bare hands rigorously pound, mash or rub. Fingers are dipped into the sauce for a taste. Seasonings are adjusted drop by drop. The best makers of kimch'i are "old hands" literally, because Korean cooking is very much a manual-intensive labor, and the best cooks are said to have a magic touch.

No recipe book can subsitute for years of trial and error necessary to develop the tastebuds to detect subtle variations of flavor and the intution to season accordingly. In the past, all the women who married into one family learned to make kimch'i in the same kitchen with their mother-in-law. The family's distinctive flavor would be handed down through generations.

These days, fewer women have the time and space to make kimch'i in the traditional way. With nuclear families now the rule, urban households living in apartments are unable to join together for kimchang, the annual kimch'i making season during which enough batches are made to last several households all winter. (You know it's kimchang time when the price of cabbage, garlic and radish rises sharply). Kimch'i used to be stored underground in earthenware jars that aided the fermentation process, but nowadays, special containers and even refrigerators are being developed to allow modern women to make smaller batches all year round.

The easiest and quickest kimch'i to make is mul kimch'i, or water-kimch'i. Slightly sweet and very refreshing, it's the perfect complement to heavy, rich dishes. Unlike most other forms of kimch'i, this does not require fermented salt shrimp paste (chŏtkal), and is fermented within days.

entitled to 9- or 7-course meals. Commoners were limited to the 5- or 3-course meals. The three-course may not sound like much, but a menu would consist of at least rice, soup, kimch'i, three vegetable dishes, two broiled foods, and two salty condiments. Imagine then the daily fare of the royal court, and the kitchen that had to prepare it three times a day!

Of course, almost nobody has such elaborate meals everyday any more. But even a dish as simple as noodles requires side dishes that add the spice and bite that Korean food is so famous for.

Which brings us to the other half of the coin: eating. Anyone who has ever been to a Korean restaurant knows that eating is a communal ritual. The gas burner that each table comes equipped with cooks a single pot of stew or a pan of broiled meat or fish, from which everyone partakes. Friendships are sealed with the sharing of drinks, as one finishes his/her glass and passes it to another. Unsanitary? Not really; Koreans feel that sharing from a common cup or pot is the best way to share that loving feeling known as *chŏng*.

How To Make:

Pulgogi: marinated beef grilled over "fire"
Pibimbap: rice mixed with vegetables
Kimbap: rice and vegetables rolled in seaweed

A typical Korean meal includes a bowl of rice, soup, vegetables, and either fish, *tubu* (bean curd, also known as tofu) or a little meat, and of course, kimchi. The better-known dishes like *pulgogi* are not everyday fare but served on special occasions.

Since many of the ingredients that make up a typical meal are hard to find, outside of an Asian grocery, we've picked a few dishes that can be made mostly with things you'd already have on hand. Some of them need a couple of days of preparation, so plan the meal ahead. Be sure to have an experienced cook nearby if you're unfamiliar with the terms.

Because the recipes are readily adaptable to substi-tutes, you can be loose with the measurements, but read through each recipe completely before starting. Once you've made the dish several times you quickly learn to eyeball how much of some-thing you'll need. The recipes here serve four moderate appetites.

The seasonings used in almost all Korean dishes are simple and easy to find: garlic, salt, sugar, green onions, red pepper, vinegar, soy sauce, and sesame oil. You can Koreanize any dish with a bowl of dipping sauce on the side. It's easy to make. Just combine one tablespoon of soy sauce with a combination of finely chopped green onions and garlic, vinegar, sesame seeds and oil, and red pepper flakes, mixed to your taste.

Rice

To make perfect rice Korean-style you need the short-grain variety, which is preferred for its fluffy sticky taste. Wash two cups of rice, picking out stones and dark ends, and rinse. Repeat until the water runs off clear. Transfer the rice to a heavy pot (stoneware is best, but don't worry if it's not.) and press flat. Add enough water so that your hand is submerged when placed on top of the rice.

With the lid on, let the rice cook on low heat until it boils, then turn the gas down very low. Simmer for ten to fifteen minutes covered, then turn

off the heat. Allow the rice to steam until the grains are soft. Eat while hot, and save the scrapings off the bottom for a special treat called *nurungji* (loosen with hot water). This should serve 2-3.

Pulgogi

Because beef was expensive in the past, dishes like *pulgogi* and *kalbi* (marinated short ribs) were served only on special occasions. Today, a trip to a *kalbi* house is the equivalent of going out for a nice steak dinner. Fortunately, *pulgogi* is easy to make at home.

You need 2.5 kg of sliced beef sirloin, 3 tablespoons of sugar and 2 tablespoons of rice wine. The marinade is made of 4 tablespoons of soy sauce, a dash of black pepper, $1^{1/2}$ tablespoons of minced garlic, 3 tablespoons of chopped green onions, 2 tablespoons of sesame oil, and 1 tablespoon of sesame seeds.

The secret to making delicious *pulgogi* is to tenderize the meat with sugar and wine. (If you don't have rice wine, try sherry, or even cola.) Let the beef soak for half an hour. While preparing the sauce. Pour the sauce over the beef and rub so that each piece is thoroughly covered. The more

Pibimbap, boiled rice with assorted vegetables and meat.

you knead the meat in the marinade, the better it will taste. Marinate for at least an hour in the refrigerator. And that's it!

Korean restaurants use a dome-shaped grill that lets the juices drip off to the sides when frying. You can use a regular fry pan. But by all means, save the drippings. It's delicious mixed into white rice.

Pibimbap

Pibimbap is a veritable meal in a bowl. *"Pibim"* means to mix, which is how you eat the artfully, arranged layers of julienned vegetables, egg, meat and sauce over rice. It almost seems a shame to break up the lovely pinwheel effect, but the taste is defintely worth it.

Pibimbap is the representative dish of the southwestern Chŏlla-do provinces, famed for their arts, culture, and cuisine. Most Koreans, regardless of where they come from, would agree that the bounteous spread of a Chŏlla-do meal—a feast, really—is unmatched for its generosity and taste. This rice dish brings together all of the best of a Korean table.

However, not all the ingredients may be available where you live. If you're lucky, your Asian grocery might stock Chinese balloon flower root (*toraji*) or bracken (*kosari*). These vegetables sometimes come in dried forms, which are just as good after soaking. If you're using toraji, soak it in salted water to remove bitterness. Chop off the hard ends and split the roots into long, thin slivers.

The beauty of *pibimbap* is that you can substitute with almost any other vegetable. Cucumbers, spinach, carrot, Korean radish, mushrooms, watercress and other leafy vegetables—anything that can add to the mix of color and texture. Eyeball how much you'll need for four big bowls, and prepare as much rice accordingly.

Wash all vegetables. Peel and julienne all root vegetables (cut into matchstick pieces). Saute them separately in a lightly oiled pan and season with a pinch of salt and pepper. If you're using spinach, boil it briefly. Drain, and then saute as above. Leafy vegetables can just be cut into bite-sized strips.

Remove mushroom stems. Also julienne and saute. Peel the cucumber and sprinkle with salt to remove water. Cut, and saute lightly.

For protein, fry four eggs sunny side up. If you wish to add beef, slice into small strips and saute with minced garlic, chopped green onions, a few drops of soy sauce, and a couple of pinches of sugar.

Into each bowl, make a bed of rice. Arrange some of each ingredient carefully in sections radiating from the center. Top with the ground beef, and the egg.

To eat, mix all the ingredients vigorously. Add red pepper paste and sesame oil to keep everything moist.

Kimbap

Kimbap is a snack food more than anything else. It's what children pack for lunch on outings and field trips. Like *pibimbap* it's a mixed-bag meal.

You will need a square bamboo rolling mat and 8 to 10 sheets of seaweed, which should be available at any Asian or health food store that stocks Japanese ingredients. Other

delicious, but optional, items to pick up while you're there are sesame oil, *mirin* (rice vinegar) and *tanmuji,* yellow pickled radish that comes in half cylinders. If you can't get a hold of a rolling mat, improvise with several sheets of foil folded together into a square large enough for the seaweed.

Kimbap requires more rice than the usual serving because it's hard to eat only a few. Follow the steps above, but use six cups of uncooked rice. Make sure the pot is big enough to allow for expansion. In the meantime, prepare the fillings. Wash and peel two carrots and cucumbers each. Slice in half lengthwise, then again and again until each strip is about the thickness of a pencil. They should be as long as the sheet of seaweed. If not, you can always put separate strips back to back. If you're using ham, *tanmuji,* and imitation crab sticks, do the same.

Next, beat 3-4 eggs. In a non-stick or well-oiled fry pan, pour half of the egg until it coats the bottom in a thin film. Cook on low heat until the top side is almost done. Very carefully, flip it over with a turner. (Ask for help). Ease the cooked egg out of the pan and let it cool. Repeat with the remaining egg. Slice into even strips.

For a traditional taste, use beef instead of the ham or crabsticks. Brown ground beef in the same pan. Break up the meat with a fork until it crumbles and season lightly with salt and pepper. Let the fat drip off. Once the rice is done, you may want to season it. This step is not absolutely necessary, but it makes the *kimbap* more flavorful. Add to the rice while still hot three tablespoons of rice vinegar (slightly sweet) for a Japanese taste, or sesame seed oil for a nuttier, meatier one. Sesame oil is expensive, though, so you can opt to spread it on the knife for slicing at the end.

Quickly rub each sheet of seaweed between your hands to remove extra flakes. Then, lay the seaweed on the rolling mat so that it is flush with the bottom edge. Spoon out one large scoop of rice and pat down so that the entire bottom half has an even, 1 cm-thick layer of rice. In the middle of the rice, press one strip of each filling into a mound.

Now, lift the bottom edge of the rolling mat and fold it over the rice so that it is completely covered. At the same time, keep your hands cupped to form a round mold. Your fingers may have to tuck under the mat to keep

the fillings centered. Then, pressing the fingers into the base of the rolled rice, roll forward. Maintain pressure as you roll so that it keeps its cylindrical shape until the end of the sheet. Don't worry, the sticky rice will keep the roll from falling apart. Repeat the process for every seaweed sheeet.

For dessert, Koreans usually have sliced fresh fruit and herb teas. After a full meal, you'll find these great for digestion.

Coffee or Tea?

Korea has traditionally been a tea-drinking culture. The tea ceremony for which Japan is famous actually had its origins in Buddhist Korea, but because of Confucian aesthetics (and politics), the art of making and drinking green tea devolved into the simple taking of barley tea.

Green tea is indeed a stimulant, stronger than coffee, as the tea leaves are unprocessed. In tea rooms called *tabang* (which also serve as meeting places, business offices, or study rooms), green tea remains a popular choice. Other Korean teas that are popular for their therapeutic effects are *ssanghwa* tea (traditional Asian herbal medicine with a raw egg yolk) and *insam* (ginseng) tea for overall strength, *omija* (berry) tea and *yuja* (citron) tea for colds, and ginger tea for indigestion.

Coffee has become part of the modern diet by virtue of its simplicity and sociability. Many Koreans drink instant coffee with plenty of sugar and cream. Nowadays, however, people are beginning to enjoy the taste of brewed coffee and even lattés in one of the many coffee specialty shops and cafes.

Dear Reader,

We hope that this book has imparted something of the flavor of Korea. Although it is not intended to be an authoritative guide to everything you could possibly want to know about this country, it has tried to offer you a sampling. We hope it may inspire you to find out more from other sources.

At the beginning, we mentioned that 안녕 means more than "Hello!" It's also what friends say when they part. So, 안녕 !

All the Best,

The Authors

KOCIS Goes Online

The Korean Overseas Culture and Information Service currently provides on-line information on Korea on the Internet to better serve the international community and help them better understand Korea.

KOCIS operates a web site "Korea Window," which offers useful information on a variety of topics including a general overview of Korea, tourist information, current issues, and official documents.

If you would like to obtain on-line information on Korea, just log in to the host computer of your local Internet provider. Then type the following: http://www.kocis.go.kr.

The administrators at KOCIS are sure that general users will be able to find information which is both rewarding and interesting. KOCIS is also striving to collect more in-depth material which specialists and experts can use in their research on Korea.

As we enter an age of new media, Korea Window will eventually be developed into a multimedia database. Once the new technology is incorporated into Korea Window, you will be able to appreciate the scenes and sounds of Korea at your very own home.